P9-DOE-441

Shakespeare
Explained

Othello

MARK MUSSARI

INTRODUCTION BY JOSEPH SOBRAN

mc Marshall Cavendish
Benchmark
New York

Series consultant: Richard Larkin

Marshall Cavendish
99 White Plains Road
Tarrytown, New York 10591
www.marshallcavendish.us

Library of Congress Cataloging-in-Publication Data

Mussari, Mark.
Othello / by Mark Mussari.
p. cm. — (Shakespeare explained)
Includes bibliographical references and index.
Summary: "A literary analysis of the play Othello. Includes information on
the history and culture of Elizabethan England"—Provided by publisher.
ISBN 978-0-7614-3422-1
1. Shakespeare, William, 1564-1616. Othello—Juvenile literature. I.
Title.
PR2829.M87 2008
822.3'3—dc22
2008037506

Photo research by: Linda Sykes
Donald Cooper/Royal Shakespeare Company: front cover; Ian Jeffrey/istockphoto: 1;
Neven Mendrila/Shutterstock: 3; Raciro/istockphoto: 4; Art Parts RF: 6, 8, 13, 24, 25; ©Nik Wheeler/
Corbis: 11; Portraitgalerie, Schloss Ambras, Innsbruck, Austria/Erich Lessing/Art Resource,
NY: 18; AA World Travel Library/Alamy: 20; ©Hideo Kurihara/Alamy: 22; Corbis/Sygma:
27; Andrew Fox/Corbis: 30; Private Collection/The Bridgeman Art Library: 37; The Gallery
Collection/Corbis: 40; ©Columbia Pictures/The Everett Collection: 43; T. Charles Erickson: 48;
The Everett Collection: 58; Johan Persson/ArenaPAL/Topfoto/The Image Works: 62;
Colin Wiloughby/ArenaPAL/Topfoto/The Image Works: 68; The Everett Collection: 73;
Lions Gate Films: 81; Elliott Franks/ArenaPAL/Topfoto/The Image Works: 89.

Editor: Deborah Grahame
Publisher: Michelle Bisson
Art Director: Anahid Hamparian
Series Design: Kay Petronio

Printed in Malaysia
135642

Contents

Shakespeare and His World

WILLIAM SHAKESPEARE,

OFTEN NICKNAMED "THE BARD," IS, BEYOND ANY COMPARISON, THE MOST TOWERING NAME IN ENGLISH LITERATURE. MANY CONSIDER HIS PLAYS THE GREATEST EVER WRITTEN. HE STANDS OUT EVEN AMONG GENIUSES.

Yet the Bard is also closer to our hearts than lesser writers, and his tremendous reputation should neither intimidate us nor prevent us from enjoying the simple delights he offers in such abundance. It is as if he had written for each of us personally. As he himself put it, "One touch of nature makes the whole world kin."

Such tragedies as *Hamlet*, *Romeo and Juliet*, and *Macbeth* are world-famous, still performed on stage and in films. These and others have also been adapted for radio, television, opera, ballet, pantomime, novels, comic books, and other media. Two of the best ways to become familiar with them are to watch some of the many fine movies that have been made of them and to listen to recordings of them by some of the world's great actors.

Even Shakespeare's individual characters have a life of their own, like real historical figures. Hamlet is still regarded as the most challenging role ever written for an actor. Roughly as many whole books have been written about Hamlet, an imaginary character, as about actual historical figures such as Abraham Lincoln and Napoleon Bonaparte.

Shakespeare created an amazing variety of vivid characters. One of Shakespeare's most peculiar traits was that he loved his characters so much—even some of his villains and secondary or comic characters—that at times he let them run away with the play, stealing attention from his heroes and heroines.

So in *A Midsummer Night's Dream* audiences remember the absurd and lovable fool Bottom the Weaver better than the lovers who are the main characters. Romeo's friend Mercutio is more fiery and witty than Romeo himself; legend claims that Shakespeare said he had to kill Mercutio or Mercutio would have killed the play.

Shakespeare also wrote dozens of comedies and historical plays, as well as nondramatic poems. Although his tragedies are now regarded as his greatest works, he freely mixed them with comedy and history. And his sonnets are among the supreme love poems in the English language.

It is Shakespeare's mastery of the English language that keeps his words familiar to us today. Every literate person knows dramatic lines such as "Wherefore art thou Romeo?"; "My kingdom for a horse!"; "To be or not to be: that is the question"; "Friends, Romans, countrymen, lend me your ears"; and "What fools these mortals be!" Shakespeare's sonnets are noted for their sweetness: "Shall I compare thee to a summer's day?"

"I WILL WEAR MY HEART UPON MY SLEEVE"

SHAKESPEARE'S LANGUAGE

WITHOUT A DOUBT, SHAKESPEARE WAS THE GREATEST MASTER OF THE ENGLISH LANGUAGE WHO EVER LIVED. BUT JUST WHAT DOES THAT MEAN?

Shakespeare's vocabulary was huge, full of references to the Bible as well as Greek and Roman mythology. Yet his most brilliant phrases often combine very simple and familiar words:

"WHAT'S IN A NAME? THAT WHICH WE CALL A ROSE BY ANY OTHER NAME WOULD SMELL AS SWEET."

He has delighted countless millions of readers. And we know him only through his language. He has shaped modern English far more than any other writer.

Or, to put it in more personal terms, you probably quote his words several times every day without realizing it, even if you have never suspected that Shakespeare could be a source of pleasure to you.

So why do so many English-speaking readers find his language so difficult? It is our language, too, but it has changed so much that it is no longer quite the same language—nor a completely different one, either.

Shakespeare's English and ours overlap without being identical. He would have some difficulty understanding us, too! Many of our everyday words and phrases would baffle him.

Shakespeare, for example, would not know what we meant by a *car,* a *radio,* a *movie*, a *television,* a *computer,* or a *sitcom,* since these things did not even exist in his time. Our old-fashioned term *railroad train* would be unimaginable to him, far in the distant future. We would have to explain to him (if we could) what *nuclear weapons, electricity,* and *democracy* are. He would also be a little puzzled by common expressions such as *high-tech, feel the heat, approval ratings, war criminal, judgmental,* and *whoopie cushion.*

So how can we call him "the greatest master of the English language"? It might seem as if he barely spoke English at all! (He would, however, recognize much of our dirty slang, even if he pronounced it slightly differently. His plays also contain many racial insults to Jews, Africans, Italians, Irish, and others. Today he would be called "insensitive.")

Many of the words of Shakespeare's time have become archaic. Words like *thou, thee, thy, thyself,* and *thine,* which were among the most common words in the language in Shakespeare's day, have all but disappeared today. We simply say *you* for both singular and plural, formal and familiar. Most other modern languages have kept their *thou.*

Sometimes the same words now have different meanings. We are apt to be misled by such simple, familiar words as *kind, wonderful, waste, just,* and *dear,* which he often uses in ways that differ from our usage.

Shakespeare also doesn't always use the words we expect to hear, the words that we ourselves would naturally use. When we might automatically say, "I beg your pardon" or just "Sorry," he might say, "I cry you mercy."

Often a glossary and footnotes will solve all three of these problems for us. But it is most important to bear in mind that Shakespeare was often hard for his first audiences to understand. Even in his own time his rich language was challenging. And this was deliberate. Shakespeare was inventing his own kind of English. It remains unique today.

A child doesn't learn to talk by using a dictionary. Children learn first by sheer immersion. We teach babies by pointing at things and saying their names. Yet the toddler always learns faster than we can teach! Even as babies we are geniuses. Dictionaries can help us later, when we already speak and read the language well (and learn more slowly).

So the best way to learn Shakespeare is not to depend on the footnotes and glossary too much, but instead to be like a baby: just get into the flow of the language. Go to performances of the plays or watch movies of them.

THE LANGUAGE HAS A MAGICAL WAY OF TEACHING ITSELF, IF WE LET IT. THERE IS NO REASON TO FEEL STUPID OR FRUSTRATED WHEN IT DOESN'T COME EASILY.

Hundreds of phrases have entered the English language from *Hamlet* alone, including "to hold, as t'were, the mirror up to nature"; "murder most foul"; "the thousand natural shocks that flesh is heir to"; "flaming youth"; "a countenance more in sorrow than in anger"; "the play's the thing"; "neither a borrower nor a lender be"; "in my mind's eye"; "something is rotten in the state of Denmark"; "alas, poor Yorick"; and "the lady doth protest too much, methinks."

From other plays we get the phrases "star-crossed lovers"; "what's in a name?"; "we have scotched the snake, not killed it"; "one fell swoop"; "it was Greek to me;" "I come to bury Caesar, not to praise him"; and "the most unkindest cut of all"—all these are among our household words. In fact, Shakespeare even gave us the expression "household words." No wonder his contemporaries marveled at his "fine filed phrase" and swooned at the "mellifluous and honey-tongued Shakespeare."

Shakespeare's words seem to combine music, magic, wisdom, and humor:

"THE COURSE OF TRUE LOVE NEVER DID RUN SMOOTH."

"HE JESTS AT SCARS THAT NEVER FELT A WOUND."

"THE FAULT, DEAR BRUTUS, IS NOT IN OUR STARS, BUT IN OURSELVES, THAT WE ARE UNDERLINGS."

"COWARDS DIE MANY TIMES BEFORE THEIR DEATHS; THE VALIANT NEVER TASTE OF DEATH BUT ONCE."

"NOT THAT I LOVED CAESAR LESS, BUT THAT I LOVED ROME MORE."

"THERE ARE MORE THINGS IN HEAVEN AND EARTH, HORATIO, THAN ARE DREAMT OF IN YOUR PHILOSOPHY."

"BREVITY IS THE SOUL OF WIT."

"THERE'S A DIVINITY THAT SHAPES OUR ENDS, ROUGH-HEW THEM HOW WE WILL."

Four centuries after Shakespeare lived, to speak English is to quote him. His huge vocabulary and linguistic fertility are still astonishing. He has had a powerful effect on all of us, whether we realize it or not. We may wonder how it is even possible for a single human being to say so many memorable things.

Only the King James translation of the Bible, perhaps, has had a more profound and pervasive influence on the English language than Shakespeare. And, of course, the Bible was written by many authors over many centuries, and the King James translation, published in 1611, was the combined effort of many scholars.

EARLY LIFE

So who, exactly, was Shakespeare? Mystery surrounds his life, largely because few records were kept during his time. Some people have even doubted his identity, arguing that the real author of Shakespeare's plays must have been a man of superior formal education and wide experience. In a sense such doubts are a natural and understandable reaction to his rare, almost miraculous powers of expression, but some people feel that the doubts themselves show a lack of respect for the supremely human poet.

Most scholars agree that Shakespeare was born in the town of Stratford-upon-Avon in the county of Warwickshire, England, in April 1564. He was baptized, according to local church records, Gulielmus (William) Shakspere (the name was spelled in several different ways) on April 26 of that year. He was one of several children, most of whom died young.

His father, John Shakespeare (or Shakspere), was a glove maker and, at times, a town official. He was often in debt or being fined for unknown delinquencies, perhaps failure to attend church regularly. It is suspected that John was a "recusant" (secret and illegal) Catholic, but there is no proof. Many

scholars have found Catholic tendencies in Shakespeare's plays, but whether Shakespeare was Catholic or not we can only guess.

At the time of Shakespeare's birth, England was torn by religious controversy and persecution. The country had left the Roman Catholic Church during the reign of King Henry VIII, who had died in 1547. Two of Henry's children, Edward and Mary, ruled after his death. When his daughter Elizabeth I became queen in 1558, she upheld his claim that the monarch of England was also head of the English Church.

Did William attend the local grammar school? He was probably entitled to, given his father's prominence in Stratford, but again, we face a frustrating absence of proof, and many people of the time learned to read very well without schooling. If he went to the town school, he would also have learned the rudiments of Latin.

We know very little about the first half of William's life. In 1582, when he was eighteen, he married Anne Hathaway, eight years his senior. Their first daughter, Susanna, was born six months later. The following year they had twins, Hamnet and Judith.

At this point William disappears from the records again. By the early 1590s we find "William Shakespeare" in London, a member of the city's leading acting company, called the Lord Chamberlain's Men. Many of Shakespeare's greatest roles, we are told, were first performed by the company's star, Richard Burbage.

Curiously, the first work published under (and identified with) Shakespeare's name was not a play but a long erotic poem, *Venus and Adonis*, in 1593. It was dedicated to the young Earl of Southampton, Henry Wriothesley.

Venus and Adonis was a spectacular success, and Shakespeare was immediately hailed as a major poet. In 1594 he dedicated a longer, more serious poem to Southampton, *The Rape of Lucrece*. It was another hit, and for many years, these two poems were considered Shakespeare's greatest works, despite the popularity of his plays.

WHO STEALS MY PURSE STEALS TRASH

SHAKESPEARE ON FILM: A SAMPLER

TODAY MOVIES, NOT LIVE PLAYS, ARE THE MORE POPULAR ART FORM. FORTUNATELY MOST OF SHAKESPEARE'S PLAYS HAVE BEEN FILMED, AND THE BEST OF THESE MOVIES OFFER AN EXCELLENT WAY TO MAKE THE BARD'S ACQUAINTANCE. RECENTLY, KENNETH BRANAGH HAS BECOME A RESPECTED CONVERTER OF SHAKESPEARE'S PLAYS INTO FILM.

Hamlet

Hamlet, Shakespeare's most famous play, has been well filmed several times. In 1948 Laurence Olivier won three Academy Awards—for best picture, best actor, and best director—for his version of the play. The film allowed him to show some of the magnetism that made him famous on the stage. Nobody spoke Shakespeare's lines more thrillingly.

The young Derek Jacobi played Hamlet in a 1980 BBC production of the play, with Patrick Stewart (now best known for *Star Trek, the Next Generation*) as the guilty king. Jacobi, like Olivier, has a gift for speaking the lines freshly; he never seems to be merely reciting the famous and familiar words. But whereas Olivier has animal passion, Jacobi is more intellectual. It is fascinating to compare the ways these two outstanding actors play Shakespeare's most complex character.

Franco Zeffirelli's 1990 *Hamlet*, starring Mel Gibson, is fascinating in a different way. Gibson, of course, is best known as an action hero, and he is not well suited to this supremely witty and introspective role, but Zeffirelli cuts the text drastically, and the result turns *Hamlet* into something that few people would have expected: a short, swift-moving action movie. Several of the other characters are brilliantly played.

Henry IV, Part One

The 1979 BBC Shakespeare series production does a commendable job in this straightforward approach to the play. Battle scenes are effective despite obvious restrictions in an indoor studio setting. Anthony Quayle gives jovial Falstaff a darker edge, and Tim Pigott-Smith's Hotspur is buoyed by some humor. Jon Finch plays King Henry IV with noble authority, and David Gwillim gives Hal a surprisingly successful transformation from boy prince to heir apparent.

Julius Caesar

No really good movie of *Julius Caesar* exists, but the 1953 film, with Marlon Brando as Mark Antony, will do. James Mason is a thoughtful Brutus, and John Gielgud, then ranked with Laurence Olivier among the greatest Shakespearean actors, plays the villainous Cassius. The film is rather dull, and Brando is out of place in a Roman toga, but it is still worth viewing.

Macbeth

Roman Polanski is best known as a director of thrillers and horror films, so it may seem natural that he should have done his 1971 *The Tragedy of Macbeth* as an often-gruesome slasher flick. But this is also one of the most vigorous of all Shakespeare films. Macbeth and his wife are played by Jon Finch and Francesca Annis, neither known for playing Shakespeare, but they are young and attractive in roles that are usually given to older actors, which gives the story a fresh flavor.

The Merchant of Venice

Once again the matchless Sir Laurence Olivier delivers a great performance as Shylock with his wife Joan Plowright as Portia in the 1974 TV film, adapted from the 1970 National Theater (of Britain) production. A 1980 BBC offering features Warren Mitchell as Shylock and Gemma Jones as Portia, with John Rhys-Davies as Salerio. The most recent production, starring Al Pacino as Shylock, Jeremy Irons as Antonio, and Joseph Fiennes as Bassanio, was filmed in Venice and released in 2004.

A Midsummer Night's Dream

Because of the prestige of his tragedies, we tend to forget how many comedies Shakespeare wrote—nearly twice the number of tragedies. Of these perhaps the most popular has always been the enchanting, atmospheric, and very silly masterpiece *A Midsummer Night's Dream*.

In more recent times several films have been made of *A Midsummer Night's Dream*. Among the more notable have been Max Reinhardt's 1935 black-and-white version, with Mickey Rooney (then a child star) as Puck.

Of the several film versions, the one starring Kevin Kline as Bottom and Stanley Tucci as Puck, made in 1999 with nineteenth-century costumes and directed by Michael Hoffman, ranks among the finest, and is surely one of the most sumptuous to watch.

Othello

Orson Welles did a budget European version in 1952, now available as a restored DVD. Laurence Olivier's 1965 film performance is predictably remarkable, though it has been said that he would only approach the part by honoring, even emulating, Paul Robeson's definitive interpretation that ran on Broadway in 1943. (Robeson was the first black actor to play Othello, the Moor of Venice, and he did so to critical acclaim, though sadly his performance was never filmed.) Maggie Smith plays a formidable Desdemona opposite Olivier, and her youth and energy will surprise younger audiences who know her only from the Harry Potter films. Laurence Fishburne brilliantly portrayed Othello in the 1995 film, costarring with Kenneth Branagh as a surprisingly human Iago, though Irène Jacob's Desdemona was disappointingly weak.

Romeo and Juliet

This, the world's most famous love story, has been filmed many times, twice very successfully over the last generation. Franco Zeffirelli directed a hit version in 1968 with Leonard Whiting and the rapturously pretty Olivia Hussey, set in Renaissance Italy. Baz Luhrmann made a much more contemporary version, with a loud rock score, starring Leonardo Di Caprio and Claire Danes, in 1996.

It seems safe to say that Shakespeare would have preferred Zeffirelli's movie, with its superior acting and rich, romantic, sun-drenched Italian scenery.

The Tempest

A 1960 Hallmark Hall of Fame production featured Maurice Evans as Prospero, Lee Remick as Miranda, Roddy McDowall as Ariel, and Richard Burton as Caliban. The special effects are primitive and the costumes are ludicrous, but it moves along at a fast pace. Another TV version aired in 1998 and was nominated for a Golden Globe. Peter Fonda played Gideon Prosper, and Katherine Heigl played his daughter Miranda Prosper. Sci-fi fans may already know that the classic 1956 film *Forbidden Planet* is modeled on themes and characters from the play.

Twelfth Night

Trevor Nunn adapted the play for the 1996 film he also directed in a rapturous Edwardian setting, with big names like Helena Bonham Carter, Richard E. Grant, Imogen Stubbs, and Ben Kingsley as Feste. A 2003 film set in modern Britain provides an interesting multicultural experience; it features an Anglo-Indian cast with Parminder Nagra (*Bend It Like Beckham*) playing Viola. For the truly intrepid, a twelve-minute silent film made in 1910 does a fine job of capturing the play through visual gags and over-the-top gesturing.

THESE FILMS HAVE BEEN SELECTED FOR SEVERAL QUALITIES: APPEAL AND ACCESSIBILITY TO MODERN AUDIENCES, EXCELLENCE IN ACTING, PACING, VISUAL BEAUTY, AND, OF COURSE, FIDELITY TO SHAKESPEARE. THEY ARE THE MOTION PICTURES WE JUDGE MOST LIKELY TO HELP STUDENTS UNDERSTAND THE SOURCE OF THE BARD'S LASTING POWER.

Today we sometimes speak of "live entertainment." In Shakespeare's day, of course, all entertainment was live, because recordings, films, television, and radio did not yet exist. Even printed books were a novelty.

In fact, most communication in those days was difficult. Transportation was not only difficult but slow, chiefly by horse and boat. Most people were illiterate peasants who lived on farms that they seldom left; cities grew up along waterways and were subject to frequent plagues that could wipe out much of the population within weeks.

Money—in coin form, not paper—was scarce and hardly existed outside the cities. By today's standards, even the rich were poor. Life was precarious. Most children died young, and famine or disease might kill anyone at any time. Everyone was familiar with death. Starvation was not rare or remote, as it is to most of us today. Medical care was poor and might kill as many people as it healed.

ELIZABETH I, A GREAT PATRON OF POETRY AND THE THEATER, WROTE SONNETS AND TRANSLATED CLASSIC WORKS.

This was the grim background of Shakespeare's theater during the reign of Queen Elizabeth I, who ruled from 1558 until her death in 1603. During that period England was also torn by religious conflict, often violent, among Roman Catholics who were loyal to the Pope, adherents of the Church of England who were loyal to the queen, and the Puritans who would take over the country in the revolution of 1642.

Under these conditions, most forms of entertainment were luxuries that were out of most people's reach. The only way to hear music was to be in the actual physical presence of singers or musicians with their instruments, which were primitive by our standards.

One brutal form of entertainment, popular in London, was bear-baiting. A bear was blinded and chained to a stake, where fierce dogs called mastiffs were turned loose to tear him apart. The theaters had to compete with the bear gardens, as they were called, for spectators.

The Puritans, or radical Protestants, objected to bear-baiting and tried to ban it. Despite their modern reputation, the Puritans were anything but conservative. Conservative people, attached to old customs, hated them. They seemed to upset everything. (Many of America's first settlers, such as the Pilgrims who came over on the *Mayflower*, were dissidents who were fleeing the Church of England.)

Plays were extremely popular, but they were primitive, too. They had to be performed outdoors in the afternoon because of the lack of indoor lighting. Often the "theater" was only an enclosed courtyard. Probably the versions of Shakespeare's plays that we know today were not used in full, but shortened to about two hours for actual performance.

But eventually more regular theaters were built, featuring a raised stage extending into the audience. Poorer spectators (illiterate "groundlings") stood on the ground around it, at times exposed to rain and snow. Wealthier people sat in raised tiers above. Aside from some costumes, there were few props or special effects and almost no scenery. Much had to be imagined: Whole battles might be represented by a few actors with swords. Thunder might be simulated by rattling a sheet of tin offstage.

The plays were far from realistic and, under the conditions of the time, could hardly try to be. Above the rear of the main stage was a small balcony. (It was this balcony from which Juliet spoke to Romeo.) Ghosts and witches might appear by entering through a trapdoor in the stage floor.

Unlike the modern theater, Shakespeare's Globe Theater—he describes it as "this wooden O"—had no curtain separating the stage from the audience. This allowed intimacy between the players and the spectators.

THE RECONSTRUCTED GLOBE THEATER WAS COMPLETED IN 1997 AND IS LOCATED IN LONDON, JUST 200 YARDS (183 METERS) FROM THE SITE OF THE ORIGINAL.

"FRAMED TO MAKE WOMEN FALSE."

The spectators probably reacted rowdily to the play, not listening in reverent silence. After all, they had come to have fun! And few of them were scholars. Again, a play had to amuse people who could not read.

The lines of plays were written and spoken in prose or, more often, in a form of verse called iambic pentameter (ten syllables with five stresses per line). There was no attempt at modern realism. Only males were allowed on the stage, so some of the greatest women's roles ever written had to be played by boys or men. (The same is true, by the way, of the ancient Greek theater.)

Actors had to be versatile, skilled not only in acting, but also in fencing, singing, dancing, and acrobatics. Within its limitations, the theater offered a considerable variety of spectacles.

Plays were big business, not yet regarded as high art, sponsored by important and powerful people (the queen loved them as much as the groundlings did). The London acting companies also toured and performed in the provinces. When plagues struck London, the government might order the theaters to be closed to prevent the spread of disease among crowds. (They remained empty for nearly two years from 1593 to 1594.)

As the theater became more popular, the Puritans grew as hostile to it as they were to bear-baiting. Plays, like books, were censored by the government, and the Puritans fought to increase restrictions, eventually banning any mention of God and other sacred topics on the stage.

In 1642 the Puritans shut down all the theaters in London, and in 1644 they had the Globe demolished. The theaters remained closed until Charles's son King Charles II was restored to the throne in 1660 and the hated Puritans were finally vanquished.

But, by then, the tradition of Shakespeare's theater had been fatally interrupted. His plays remained popular, but they were often rewritten by inferior dramatists and it was many years before they were performed (again) as he had originally written them.

THE ROYAL SHAKESPEARE THEATER, IN STRATFORD-UPON-AVON, WAS CLOSED IN 2007. A NEWLY DESIGNED INTERIOR WITH A 1000-SEAT AUDITORIUM WILL BE COMPLETED IN 2010.

Today, of course, the plays are performed both in theaters and in films, sometimes in costumes of the period (ancient Rome for *Julius Caesar*, medieval England for *Henry V*), sometimes in modern dress (*Richard III* has recently been reset in England in the 1930s).

PLAYS

In the England of Queen Elizabeth I, plays were enjoyed by all classes of people, but they were not yet respected as a serious form of art.

Shakespeare's plays began to appear in print in individual, or "quarto," editions in 1594, but none of these bore his name until 1598. Although his tragedies are now ranked as his supreme achievements, his name was first associated with comedies and with plays about English history.

The dates of Shakespeare's plays are notoriously hard to determine. Few performances of them were documented; some were not printed until decades after they first appeared on the stage. Mainstream scholars generally place most of the comedies and histories in the 1590s, admitting that this time frame is no more than a widely accepted estimate.

The three parts of *King Henry VI*, culminating in a fourth part, *Richard III*, deal with the long and complex dynastic struggle or civil wars known as the Wars of the Roses (1455–1487), one of England's most turbulent periods. Today it is not easy to follow the plots of these plays.

It may seem strange to us that a young playwright should have written such demanding works early in his career, but they were evidently very popular with the Elizabethan public. Of the four, only *Richard III*, with its wonderfully villainous starring role, is still often performed.

Even today, one of Shakespeare's early comedies, *The Taming of the Shrew*, remains a crowd-pleaser. (It has enjoyed success in a 1999 film adaptation, *10 Things I Hate About You*, with Heath Ledger and Julia Stiles.)

AROUND 1850 DOUBTS STARTED TO SURFACE ABOUT WHO HAD ACTUALLY WRITTEN SHAKESPEARE'S PLAYS, CHIEFLY BECAUSE MANY OTHER AUTHORS, SUCH AS MARK TWAIN, THOUGHT THE PLAYS' AUTHOR WAS TOO WELL EDUCATED AND KNOWLEDGEABLE TO HAVE BEEN THE MODESTLY SCHOOLED MAN FROM STRATFORD.

Who, then, was the real author? Many answers have been given, but the three leading candidates are Francis Bacon, Christopher Marlowe, and Edward de Vere, Earl of Oxford.

Francis Bacon (1561–1626)

Bacon was a distinguished lawyer, scientist, philosopher, and essayist. Many considered him one of the great geniuses of his time, capable of any literary achievement, though he wrote little poetry and, as far as we know, no dramas. When people began to suspect that "Shakespeare" was only a pen name, he seemed like a natural candidate. But his writing style was vastly different from the style of the plays.

Christopher Marlowe (1564–1593)

Marlowe wrote several excellent tragedies in a style much like that of the Shakespeare tragedies, though without the comic blend. But he was reportedly killed in a mysterious incident in 1593, before most of the Bard's plays existed. Could his death have been faked? Is it possible that he lived on for decades in hiding, writing under a pen name? This is what his advocates contend.

Edward de Vere, Earl of Oxford (1550–1604)

Oxford is now the most popular and plausible alternative to the lad from Stratford. He had a high reputation as a poet and playwright in his day, but his life was full of scandal. That controversial life seems to match what the poet says about himself in the sonnets, as well as many events in the plays (especially *Hamlet*). However, he died in 1604, and most scholars believe this rules him out as the author of plays that were published after that date.

THE GREAT MAJORITY OF EXPERTS REJECT THESE AND ALL OTHER ALTERNATIVE CANDIDATES, STICKING WITH THE TRADITIONAL VIEW, AFFIRMED IN THE 1623 FIRST FOLIO OF THE PLAYS, THAT THE AUTHOR WAS THE MAN FROM STRATFORD. THAT REMAINS THE SAFEST POSITION TO TAKE, UNLESS STARTLING NEW EVIDENCE TURNS UP, WHICH, AT THIS LATE DATE, SEEMS HIGHLY UNLIKELY.

The story is simple: The enterprising Petruchio resolves to marry a rich young woman, Katherina Minola, for her wealth, despite her reputation for having a bad temper. Nothing she does can discourage this dauntless suitor, and the play ends with Kate becoming a submissive wife. It is all the funnier for being unbelievable.

With *Romeo and Juliet* the Bard created his first enduring triumph. This tragedy of "star-crossed lovers" from feuding families is known around the world. Even people with only the vaguest knowledge of Shakespeare are often aware of this universally beloved story. It has inspired countless similar stories and adaptations, such as the hit musical *West Side Story*.

By the mid-1590s Shakespeare was successful and prosperous, a partner in the Lord Chamberlain's Men. He was rich enough to buy New Place, one of the largest houses in his hometown of Stratford.

Yet, at the peak of his good fortune, came the worst sorrow of his life: Hamnet, his only son, died in August 1596 at the age of eleven, leaving nobody to carry on his family name, which was to die out with his two daughters.

Our only evidence of his son's death is a single line in the parish burial register. As far as we know, this crushing loss left no mark on Shakespeare's work. As far as his creative life shows, it was as if nothing had happened. His silence about his grief may be the greatest puzzle of his mysterious life, although, as we shall see, others remain.

During this period, according to traditional dating (even if it must be somewhat hypothetical), came the torrent of Shakespeare's mightiest works. Among these was another quartet of English history plays, this one centering on the legendary King Henry IV, including *Richard II* and the two parts of *Henry IV*.

Then came a series of wonderful romantic comedies: *Much Ado About Nothing*, *As You Like It*, and *Twelfth Night*.

ACTOR JOSEPH FIENNES PORTRAYED THE BARD IN THE 1998 FILM *SHAKESPEARE IN LOVE.* DIRECTED BY JOHN MADDEN.

In 1598 the clergyman Francis Meres, as part of a larger work, hailed Shakespeare as the English Ovid, supreme in love poetry as well as drama. "The Muses would speak with Shakespeare's fine filed phrase," Meres wrote, "if they would speak English." He added praise of Shakespeare's "sugared sonnets among his private friends." It is tantalizing; Meres seems to know something of the poet's personal life, but he gives us no hard information. No wonder biographers are frustrated.

Next the Bard returned gloriously to tragedy with *Julius Caesar*. In the play Caesar has returned to Rome in great popularity after his military triumphs.

Brutus and several other leading senators, suspecting that Caesar means to make himself king, plot to assassinate him. Midway through the play, after the assassination, comes one of Shakespeare's most famous scenes. Brutus speaks at Caesar's funeral. But then Caesar's friend Mark Antony delivers a powerful attack on the conspirators, inciting the mob to fury. Brutus and the others, forced to flee Rome, die in the ensuing civil war. In the end the spirit of Caesar wins after all. If Shakespeare had written nothing after *Julius Caesar*, he would still have been remembered as one of the greatest playwrights of all time. But his supreme works were still to come.

Only Shakespeare could have surpassed *Julius Caesar*, and he did so with *Hamlet* (usually dated about 1600). King Hamlet of Denmark has died, apparently bitten by a poisonous snake. Claudius, his brother, has married the dead king's widow, Gertrude, and become the new king, to the disgust and horror of Prince Hamlet. The ghost of old Hamlet appears to young Hamlet, reveals that he was actually poisoned by Claudius, and demands revenge. Hamlet accepts this as his duty, but cannot bring himself to kill his hated uncle. What follows is Shakespeare's most brilliant and controversial plot.

The story of *Hamlet* is set against the religious controversies of the Bard's time. Is the ghost in hell or purgatory? Is Hamlet Catholic or Protestant? Can revenge ever be justified? We are never really given the answers to such questions. But the play reverberates with them.

THE KING'S MEN

In 1603 Queen Elizabeth I died, and King James VI of Scotland became King James I of England. He also became the patron of Shakespeare's acting company, so the Lord Chamberlain's Men became the King's Men. From this point on, we know less of Shakespeare's life in London than in Stratford, where he kept acquiring property.

In the later years of the sixteenth century Shakespeare had been a rather elusive figure in London, delinquent in paying taxes. From 1602 to 1604 he lived, according to his own later testimony, with a French immigrant family named Mountjoy. After 1604 there is no record of any London residence for Shakespeare, nor do we have any reliable recollection of him or his whereabouts by others. As always, the documents leave much to be desired.

Nearly as great as *Hamlet* is *Othello*, and many regard *King Lear*, the heart-breaking tragedy about an old king and his three daughters, as Shakespeare's supreme tragedy. Shakespeare's shortest tragedy, *Macbeth*, tells the story of a Scottish lord and his wife who plot to murder the king of Scotland to gain the throne for themselves. *Antony and Cleopatra*, a sequel to *Julius Caesar*, depicts the aging Mark Antony in love with the enchanting queen of Egypt. *Coriolanus*, another Roman tragedy, is the poet's least popular masterpiece.

SONNETS AND THE END

The year 1609 saw the publication of Shakespeare's Sonnets. Of these 154 puzzling love poems, the first 126 are addressed to a handsome young man, unnamed, but widely believed to be the Earl of Southampton; the rest concern a dark woman, also unidentified. These mysteries are still debated by scholars.

Near the end of his career Shakespeare turned to comedy again, but it was a comedy of a new and more serious kind. Magic plays a large role in these late plays. For example, in *The Tempest*, the exiled duke of Milan, Prospero, uses magic to defeat his enemies and bring about a final reconciliation.

According to the most commonly accepted view, Shakespeare, not yet fifty, retired to Stratford around 1610. He died prosperous in 1616, and left a will that divided his goods, with a famous provision leaving his wife "my second-best bed." He was buried in the chancel of the parish church, under a tombstone bearing a crude rhyme:

GOOD FRIEND, FOR JESUS SAKE FORBEARE
TO DIG THE DUST ENCLOSED HERE.
BLEST BE THE MAN THAT SPARES THESE STONES,
AND CURSED BE HE THAT MOVES MY BONES.

This epitaph is another hotly debated mystery: Did the great poet actually compose these lines himself?

GOOD FREND FOR IESVS SAKE FORBEARE,
TO DIGG HE DVST ENCLOASED HEARE.
BLESE BE Y MAN Y SPARES HES STONES,
AND CVRST BE HE Y MOVES MY BONES.

SHAKESPEARE'S GRAVE IN HOLY TRINITY CHURCH, STRATFORD-UPON-AVON. HIS WIFE, ANNE HATHAWAY, IS BURIED BESIDE HIM.

THE FOLIO

In 1623 Shakespeare's colleagues of the King's Men produced a large volume of the plays (excluding the sonnets and other poems) titled *The Comedies, Histories, and Tragedies of Mr. William Shakespeare* with a woodcut portrait—the only known portrait—of the Bard. As a literary monument it is priceless, containing our only texts of half the plays; as a source of biographical information it is severely disappointing, giving not even the dates of Shakespeare's birth and death.

Ben Jonson, then England's poet laureate, supplied a long prefatory poem saluting Shakespeare as the equal of the great classical Greek tragedians Aeschylus, Sophocles, and Euripides, adding that "He was not of an age, but for all time."

Some would later denigrate Shakespeare. His reputation took more than a century to conquer Europe, where many regarded him as semi-barbarous. His works were not translated before 1740. Jonson himself, despite his personal affection, would deprecate "idolatry" of the Bard. For a time Jonson himself was considered more "correct" than Shakespeare, and possibly the superior artist.

But Jonson's generous verdict is now the whole world's. Shakespeare was not merely of his own age, "but for all time."

BUT THIS DENOTED A FOREGONE CONCLUSION.

A GLOSSARY OF LITERARY TERMS

allegory—a story in which characters and events stand for general moral truths. Shakespeare never uses this form simply, but his plays are full of allegorical elements.

alliteration—repetition of one or more initial sounds, especially consonants, as in the saying "through thick and thin," or in Julius Caesar's statement, "veni, vidi, vici."

allusion—a reference, especially when the subject referred to is not actually named, but is unmistakably hinted at.

aside—a short speech in which a character speaks to the audience, unheard by other characters on the stage.

comedy—a story written to amuse, using devices such as witty dialogue (high comedy) or silly physical movement (low comedy). Most of Shakespeare's comedies were romantic comedies, incorporating lovers who endure separations, misunderstandings, and other obstacles but who are finally united in a happy resolution.

deus ex machina—an unexpected, artificial resolution to a play's convoluted plot. Literally, "god out of a machine."

dialogue—speech that takes place among two or more characters.

diction—choice of words for tone. A speech's diction may be dignified (as when a king formally addresses his court), comic (as when the ignorant grave diggers debate whether Ophelia deserves a religious funeral), vulgar, romantic, or whatever the dramatic occasion requires. Shakespeare was a master of diction.

Elizabethan—having to do with the reign of Queen Elizabeth I, from 1558 until her death in 1603. This is considered the most famous period in the history of England, chiefly because of Shakespeare and other noted authors (among them Sir Philip Sidney, Edmund Spenser, and Christopher Marlowe). It was also an era of military glory, especially the defeat of the huge Spanish Armada in 1588.

Globe—the Globe Theater housed Shakespeare's acting company, the Lord Chamberlain's Men (later known as the King's Men). Built in 1598, it caught fire and burned down during a performance of *Henry VIII* in 1613.

hyperbole—an excessively elaborate exaggeration used to create special emphasis or a comic effect, as in Montague's remark that his son Romeo's sighs are "adding to clouds more clouds" in *Romeo and Juliet*.

irony—a discrepancy between what a character says and what he or she truly believes, what is expected to happen and what really happens, or between what a character says and what others understand.

metaphor—a figure of speech in which one thing is identified with another, such as when Hamlet calls his father a "fair mountain." (See also **simile**.)

monologue—a speech delivered by a single character.

motif—a recurrent theme or image, such as disease in *Hamlet* or moonlight in *A Midsummer Night's Dream*.

oxymoron—a phrase that combines two contradictory terms, as in the phrase "sounds of silence" or Hamlet's remark, "I must be cruel only to be kind."

personification—imparting personality to something impersonal ("the sky wept"); giving human qualities to an idea or an inanimate object, as in the saying "love is blind."

pun—a playful treatment of words that sound alike, or are exactly the same, but have different meanings. In *Romeo and Juliet* Mercutio says, after being fatally wounded, "Ask for me tomorrow and you shall find me a grave man." "Grave" could mean either a place of burial or serious.

simile—a figure of speech in which one thing is compared to another, usually using the word *like* or *as*. (See also **metaphor**.)

soliloquy—a speech delivered by a single character, addressed to the audience. The most famous are those of Hamlet, but Shakespeare uses this device frequently to tell us his characters' inner thoughts.

symbol—a visible thing that stands for an invisible quality, as poison in *Hamlet* stands for evil and treachery.

syntax—sentence structure or grammar. Shakespeare displays amazing variety of syntax, from the sweet simplicity of his songs to the clotted fury of his great tragic heroes, who can be very difficult to understand at a first hearing. These effects are deliberate; if we are confused, it is because Shakespeare means to confuse us.

theme—the abstract subject or message of a work of art, such as revenge in *Hamlet* or overweening ambition in *Macbeth*.

tone—the style or approach of a work of art. The tone of *A Midsummer Night's Dream*, set by the lovers, Bottom's crew, and the fairies, is light and sweet. The tone of *Macbeth*, set by the witches, is dark and sinister.

tragedy—a story that traces a character's fall from power, sanity, or privilege. Shakespeare's well-known tragedies include *Hamlet, Macbeth,* and *Othello*.

tragicomedy—a story that combines elements of both tragedy and comedy, moving a heavy plot through twists and turns to a happy ending.

verisimilitude—having the appearance of being real or true.

understatement—a statement expressing less than intended, often with an ironic or comic intention; the opposite of hyperbole.

SHAKESPEARE AND
OTHELLO

A lobby card advertising the ▶
1952 film directed by and
starring Orson Welles

CHAPTER ONE

Shakespeare and Othello

OTHELLO, THE MOOR OF VENICE IS THE MOST TIGHTLY CONSTRUCTED OF SHAKESPEARE'S TRAGEDIES AND, IN MANY WAYS, THE MOST MODERN. WHAT WERE ONCE CONSIDERED MINOR ELEMENTS IN THE DRAMA—ISSUES OF RACE, GENDER, AND CLASS—HAVE BECOME ITS MAIN CONCERNS FOR BOTH AUDIENCES AND CRITICS. ONE MODERN SHAKESPEAREAN CRITIC HAS CALLED *OTHELLO* "THE TRAGEDY OF CHOICE" FOR THE CURRENT GENERATION.

Othello features one of Shakespeare's smallest casts. This narrow focus, especially on the three main characters—the African general Othello, his white Venetian wife, Desdemona, and his devious ensign Iago—draws both audiences and readers even closer to the tragedy at hand. In fact one or more of these three characters are on stage for all but one of the play's fifteen scenes.

Othello's limited time frame also intensifies the play's sparse, modern effect. The Bard's other tragedies, including *Hamlet, Macbeth,* and *King Lear,* span months—even years—of time. In *Othello,* however, Shakespeare presents only two or three days and nights in the lives of his characters.

Shakespeare's main source for *Othello* was an Italian tale by Giovanni Battista Giraldi (also known as Cinthio). In Giraldi's original work, first published in 1565, a beautiful Venetian woman named Disdemona marries a North African captain referred to only as "the Moor." Because she has previously rejected the Moor's ensign, he convinces the captain that she has been unfaithful and plays on the Moor's unease about his race. Later in Giraldi's story the Moor and his ensign murder Disdemona; her relatives ultimately avenge her death. As *Othello* reveals, Shakespeare breathes a much deeper life into this melodramatic plot.

Some scholars have traced the influence of another play, *The Tragical History of Dr. Faustus,* by Shakespeare's contemporary Christopher Marlowe. Written around 1589, *Dr. Faustus* tells the story of a magician who sells his soul to the devil to obtain complete knowledge, but ends up with nothing. The closeness between the characters of Othello and Iago seems to parallel that between Faustus and his devil in Marlowe's play.

The issue of race continues to spur debate about *Othello* and makes the play ripe for modern interpretations. From the opening scene, the

"I SAW OTHELLO'S VISAGE IN HIS MIND."

AN 1850 PAINTING BY
THEODORE CHASSERIAU, *OTHELLO
AND DESDEMONA IN VENICE*

interracial marriage between Othello and Desdemona colors all aspects of the play. Race also provides further motivation for the resentful Iago to destroy the general's happiness. His insults often turn on the relationship between the black Moor and his white wife.

Modern audiences must remember that Elizabethan England had few immigrants or people of color. North African Moors—and in particular the darker-skinned ones—would probably have been feared in Shakespeare's day, especially because many were Muslims. At times Shakespeare's characters and their words reflect the stereotypes of his age, yet he often manages to make his characters more three-dimensional and human. This is certainly the case with Othello, one of the Bard's most complex creations.

Issues about colonialism and the culture clash that often follows have also surfaced in more recent productions. A number of European countries sold African natives into slavery. Although this aspect of colonialism does not appear to be Shakespeare's main concern, Othello does refer to being sold into slavery in his youth. The Venetian colony of Cyprus also serves as a plot device and one of the play's main settings. Shakespeare uses these two settings to draw contrasts between the cultured city-state of Venice and its wilder colony at Cyprus.

Modern audiences will also savor one of Shakespeare's finest creations, the villainous Iago. In no other play has Shakespeare concentrated evil in such a blatantly wicked character. Whereas the general Othello is a man of action, Shakespeare crafts a master of rhetoric, a manipulator of language, in Iago. Over the centuries the character has become the prototype for many villains in both literature and film.

Most scholars date the Bard's writing of *Othello* around 1603–1604. A record exists of the play being performed by the King's Men at Court on November 1, 1604. Two versions of the play's text exist. One is the shorter quarto (a small individual edition) dated 1622, and the other appears in the great Folio of Shakespeare's plays from 1623. The Folio version is longer, by about 160 lines, and it often serves as the basis for most current editions.

THE PLAY'S THE THING

- OVERVIEW AND ANALYSIS

- LIST OF CHARACTERS

- ANALYSIS OF MAJOR CHARACTERS

A poster features Laurence ▶
Fishburne as Othello and
Irene Jacob as Desdemona
in the 1995 film.

laurence
FISHBURNE

irene
JACOB

kenneth
BRANAGH

Othello

Chapter
Two

66929   66929

The Play's the Thing

ACT I, SCENE 1

OVERVIEW

Othello opens with a night scene as two men, Iago and Roderigo, meet on the streets of Venice. Iago admits his hatred for his general, the Moor Othello, who has made Iago an ensign and given the desired post of lieutenant to another man, Cassio. At the same time Roderigo reveals that he is angry because Othello has run off with Desdemona, a woman who rejected Roderigo's earlier advances.

Iago suggests that they wake Desdemona's father, the Venetian senator Brabantio, and tell him that his daughter has eloped with the black Moor. An appalled Brabantio vows to rouse the Duke of Venice and get a band of armed men to find Desdemona and Othello.

ANALYSIS

Shakespeare immediately establishes Iago as a master of persuasion who is filled with hatred for Othello. In his first long speech Iago delivers a tirade about losing the position of lieutenant and his belief that he was more suited for the position than Cassio. Iago also openly admits to being a dissembler, one who feels one way but intentionally acts another. As he tells Roderigo: "I am not what I am." In addition Iago's repeated use of the term the Moor to describe Othello indicates his awareness of Othello's skin color.

Through the dialogue Shakespeare quickly establishes the power of Iago's manipulation. Both Iago and Roderigo discuss their envious feelings—Iago for Cassio and Roderigo for Othello. Through that envy Shakespeare lays the foundation for Iago's plotting and for the play's tragedy.

Roderigo responds positively to Iago's anger for Othello and hatred for Cassio, and he readily accepts the ensign's advice. With Iago prompting Roderigo to cause a ruckus when he awakens Brabantio, the two men then set out to expose Desdemona's marriage to Othello. At first Brabantio believes Roderigo is still hurting from Desdemona's rejection, but Roderigo persuades the senator that Othello has seduced his daughter.

Shakespeare also uses the scene to inform us of the play's war plot: The Venetians have been fighting the Turks in an ongoing war over the Venetian colony at Cyprus.

ACT I, SCENE 2

Later in the night Iago and Othello meet in front of the Moor's lodgings. Iago claims that he has killed men in war, but he would never plot to murder someone—or else he would have killed Brabantio for speaking so rudely about Othello. He then tells Othello that he is worried about the influence Brabantio may have on the Duke of Venice.

Othello defends his own reputation, his royal background, and his long service to Venice. He also insists that he truly loves Desdemona or would never have risked such a negative reaction.

Othello's new lieutenant Cassio arrives with orders that the Moor is to meet with the duke and other senators who have called an emergency session to deal with the conflict in Cyprus. Just as Iago is about to tell Cassio about the general's marriage, Othello returns with Brabantio and Roderigo, along with others who are carrying torches and weapons. Swords are drawn but Othello manages to calm everyone down.

Brabantio then accuses Othello of using magic to seduce Desdemona. Othello convinces Brabantio—who wants to have him arrested—to accompany him to the Senate, where the old senator can then formally accuse Othello of being a "foul thief."

ANALYSIS

On the heels of the previous scene in which Iago openly expressed his hatred for Othello, his audacity becomes all too clear in his syrupy words of loyalty to the Moor's "honor." The embittered ensign presents himself as a man of "conscience" who would gladly kill for his general. Audiences cannot help but notice Iago's reference to the mythological Janus, a Roman god with two faces.

Othello's first speech is a rousing defense of his own character: He feels confident that he can rely on his reputation and accomplishments to persuade Brabantio. He also refers to his royal upbringing and insists that he is equal in bearing to Desdemona's family.

Cassio's arrival and summons reinforce Othello's importance in Venice. He has been "hotly called for" by the Duke, who is apparently concerned with the developing military events in Cyprus.

Brabantio's accusation that Othello has used "chains of magic" and "foul charms" to lure Desdemona to him reflects his disparaging view of Othello's race—or as he calls him: "such a thing as thou." These remarks also emphasize the view that the African Othello is exotic and must therefore be a practitioner of evil arts.

Hearing that the duke has summoned Othello in the middle of the night, a surprised Brabantio agrees to plead his case in front of the Venetian Senate.

ACT 1, SCENE 3

OVERVIEW

In the chamber of the Venetian Senate, the duke and his senators discuss different reports of the movement of the Turkish fleet and conclude that its target is the island of Cyprus. The duke decides to send Othello to take over command of the Venetian defenders, who are presently under the guidance of the less-experienced Montano.

Othello and Brabantio, along with their separate supporters, arrive to discuss the conflict over Desdemona. The duke asks for evidence of Brabantio's claims that Othello has bewitched the old man's daughter. Othello suggests that they send for Desdemona so she can explain the truth, and then he offers a full account of his courtship.

Once Desdemona arrives she confirms Othello's account of their relationship in front of her father and the senators and thereby

vindicates the Moor. The duke accepts the explanation and then commissions Othello to proceed to Cyprus. Desdemona asks if she may accompany Othello on his mission. The duke agrees, and Othello assigns the duty of transporting his wife to Iago, whom he describes as "a man . . . of honesty and trust."

Unhappy with the outcome of his plea, Brabantio leaves with a parting warning to Othello about Desdemona's deceptive nature: "She has deceived her father," he advises, "and may thee."

Once all others leave, Roderigo tells Iago that he will drown himself with grief over losing Desdemona. Assuring Roderigo that Desdemona will grow tired of Othello, Iago then convinces him to get some money and follow Desdemona to Cyprus and to use a beard to disguise himself. Roderigo exits, asserting that he will sell all his land (to acquire the necessary funds).

Left alone onstage, Iago derides Roderigo as a "fool," easily parted from his money, someone whom Iago can use for "sport and profit." He reiterates his hatred for Othello and concocts his plan to steal Cassio's place as lieutenant by convincing Othello that Cassio has been "too familiar" with Desdemona.

ANALYSIS

Shakespeare masterfully moves the action from scene to scene in Act I. In the first scene Iago and Roderigo talk about going to see Brabantio, and the second scene begins there. In the second scene Othello and Brabantio discuss going to see the duke, and the third scene begins in the duke's chamber.

The opening dialogue between the duke and his senators indicates their high opinion of Othello, who is referred to as "valiant." Othello's first self-defense follows on the heels of Brabantio's claims of "spells and medicines." Through Othello's eloquence in this speech and in the next one, Shakespeare establishes him as a general who is also in command of his words.

In his first speech Othello insists that he is merely a military man who lacks "the soft phrase of peace," a man who can only speak of "broil

I DO PERCEIVE HERE A DIVIDED DUTY.

and battle." Othello uses his self-effacing words to undercut Brabantio's claims of black magic against his daughter, claims that now seem to be wild and ridiculous.

Othello's long second speech offers a touching narrative of love as he describes his own difficult and often dangerous life and Desdemona's growing fascination with it. He has had "hairbreadth" escapes, encounters with "Cannibals" and was even "sold to slavery" by an "insolent foe." Is he also fascinating his audience? He definitely wins over the duke, whose opinion is further swayed by Desdemona's profession of love for and "duty" to Othello.

Shakespeare depicts Desdemona as a strong young woman in her first scene. In front of the duke she defies her father's wishes and insists that her loyalty belongs to her new husband, Othello. In this sense Shakespeare makes her subsequent request to accompany Othello to Cyprus—during a war, no less—believable.

By already permitting us to see Iago's true colors, Shakespeare sets up the irony of Othello leaving Desdemona in his devious ensign's care. Othello's repeated use of the word *honest* to describe Iago must surely make the audience uneasy.

In the final quarter of the scene, Shakespeare returns again to a dialogue between Iago and Roderigo. Iago's rhetoric reveals that he places no value on virtue ("a fig!"). He persuades Roderigo not to drown himself—not because he wants to save Roderigo but because he wants to use Roderigo in his plan. Iago also plays on Othello's ethnicity by suggesting that "Moors" are often "changeable" in their ways. Finally he convinces Roderigo that the misguided fool may still obtain Desdemona's affections.

If the audience still has any doubts about Iago's motivation, Shakespeare clears them up in this statement to Roderigo: "I have told thee often, and I retell thee again and again, I hate the Moor." In his closing soliloquy Iago openly hatches his plot to destroy Othello.

ACT II, SCENE 1

OVERVIEW

At a seaport in Cyprus, Montano (the governor of the island) and two Cypriot gentlemen discuss the severe storm that is raging offshore. A third gentleman reveals that the Turkish fleet has been destroyed in the storm and that Cassio has arrived. All of them are worried about Othello's safety. Cassio enters and describes Othello's marriage to Desdemona, whom he praises highly. Desdemona then arrives, along with her escort Iago, his wife, Emilia, and a disguised Roderigo.

While they all wait for Othello, Iago offers some wry observation on both his own wife and women in general. Othello finally enters, joyously greets his wife, and announces the end of the Turkish threat to Cyprus.

After the others depart, Iago sets his plot into motion by persuading the disguised Roderigo that Desdemona is really in love with Cassio. Alone, Iago decides that Emilia has been the object of both Cassio's and Othello's desire. He concludes that both he and Cassio must lust after Desdemona, thereby crafting an imaginary conflict to justify his actions.

ANALYSIS

As this scene opens, Shakespeare enlivens his stage with the noises of the storm, cannon firings, and announcements of sail sightings. Characters once again create anticipation by referring to Othello as "brave" before he enters the scene. To increase focus on the central characters and the impending personal conflict, Shakespeare quickly resolves the military conflict over Cyprus.

Perhaps Cassio's little paean to "the divine Desdemona" seems a bit over the top. Having already established Iago's intentions, the Bard has us on the lookout for any word or event that might play into Iago's hands. Iago's sarcasm about women—with both his wife and Desdemona—may also seem more sexist than humorous to modern ears.

Iago is quick to focus on Cassio's affection for Desdemona, especially when Cassio takes her warmly by the hand. Iago observes, "With as little a web as this will I ensnare as great a fly as Cassio." And we know he means it!

Othello's arrival and gracious greeting of his wife is a moment filled with joy and culminating in a kiss. Shakespeare will not stage a kiss again between the two characters until the end of the play—and under much different circumstances.

Left alone again with Roderigo, Iago unleashes his contorted reasoning to goad Roderigo into action. Iago's earlier barbs about women now blossom into a full assault on Desdemona's faithfulness. Even the easily persuaded Roderigo cannot believe Iago's claims at first. Through his rhetoric Iago convinces Roderigo that Desdemona's affections for Othello will eventually fade and be redirected toward "handsome, young" Cassio.

Can we help but be impressed by the careful genius of Iago's plotting? He directs Roderigo to provoke an argument with Cassio so that Iago can incite the lieutenant's dismissal for fighting. He also convinces Roderigo that removing Cassio will benefit him on his path toward obtaining Desdemona. In his closing soliloquy Iago announces his intention to "put the Moor/At least into a jealousy so strong/That judgment cannot cure." He claims his ultimate goal is to drive Othello "to madness."

ACT II, SCENE 2

OVERVIEW

In this mini-scene Othello's herald enters with a proclamation: The hours between five o'clock and eleven o'clock will be devoted to feasting and revelry to celebrate the destruction of the Turkish fleet and Othello and Desdemona's "nuptial." He closes with a blessing for Cyprus and for "our noble general" Othello.

ANALYSIS

The word *nuptial* in this context indicates the consummation of Othello's marriage. Such a joyous proclamation would mark the end of conflict in a comedy, but *Othello* is moving in another direction.

ACT II, SCENE 3

OVERVIEW

At the castle in Cyprus Othello asks Cassio to supervise the setting of the guard and then retires to his marriage chamber. Iago enters and persuades Cassio—who has revealed that he cannot drink—to have some wine with some other gentlemen. As Iago leads the group in some drinking songs, Cassio becomes increasingly drunk and foul-tempered. After Cassio exits, Iago tells Montano that Cassio is drunk every night.

Roderigo enters and Iago directs him to follow Cassio. Shortly thereafter, Roderigo races back in with an angry Cassio on his heels. When Montano tries to intervene, Cassio becomes violent and wounds him with a sword.

Othello and some of his men, with weapons drawn, arrive and discover that Montano is bleeding. Appalled at what has happened, Othello strips Cassio of his title of lieutenant, saying: "Cassio I love thee;/But never more be officer of mine."

Left alone with Iago, Cassio regrets his drunken behavior and the loss of his reputation. Iago then persuades Cassio that there are "ways to recover" Othello's affection. He suggests that Cassio appeal to Desdemona to plead his case to Othello in order to restore his position. After Cassio leaves,

Iago—in another soliloquy—praises the "honesty" and rationality of his advice to Cassio: Desdemona will, indeed, gladly speak for Cassio.

Iago announces that he will use all this good will between Cassio and Desdemona to his own advantage against Othello. He then comforts Roderigo and tells him to be patient now that Cassio has been disgraced. Left alone again, Iago decides to bring his wife, Emilia, into the plot.

ANALYSIS

In this scene Shakespeare reveals Iago's increasing control over the other characters. Iago behaves like a puppeteer throughout this scene, yet he is careful enough to manipulate others to act in a manner that is appropriate to their personalities. He never directly involves himself in the action. His plying of Cassio with alcohol offers the perfect setup for the drunken brawl that follows.

Iago knows that Cassio, once he drinks, will be "full of quarrel and offence." He also uses Roderigo ("my sick fool") to enact his plan of exposing Cassio's darker sides to Othello. Shakespeare leaves us no choice but to be impressed by this "villain," as Iago ironically refers to himself twice in his soliloquy. Once he sets into motion the fight between Cassio and Montano, Iago can simply sit back and act as surprised as everyone else.

Iago is a study in deception as he feigns reluctance when telling Othello what has happened—to the point that Othello actually accuses "honest" Iago of mincing his words to spare Cassio! Iago offers further proof of his diabolical nature when he then takes Cassio into his confidence, slowly convincing the dejected soldier to pursue Desdemona's help. It would be sensible advice if only it came from another source. Through these machinations, Shakespeare creates both surprise *and* inevitability in the events that follow.

In his soliloquy Iago once again reveals the wonderfully warped reasoning that drives his actions. How disturbing to discover that Shakespeare creates a villain who takes his audience into his confidence. Iago describes his ultimate purpose for prompting Cassio to ask Desdemona to appeal to Othello: He'll "pour this pestilence" into Othello's ear to convince him that the real reason Desdemona supports Cassio is that the lieutenant is her lover. Diseased thoughts, indeed!

ACT III, SCENE 1

OVERVIEW

Outside the general's quarters Cassio directs some musicians to play a morning love song for Othello and Desdemona. A clown, sent by Othello, interrupts the music with witty remarks and an offering of money (from Othello, who wants them to stop). Cassio bribes the clown to get him an audience with Emilia, but Iago offers to take care of it. Cassio is touched and comments: "I never knew/A Florentine more kind and honest." Emilia then arrives, and Cassio asks her if she can help him to see Desdemona. She happily agrees.

ANALYSIS

Shakespeare uses both the music and the clown as a diversion as the plot races toward disaster. More interesting is Emilia's arrival and subsequent involvement in Cassio's predicament. Through her we learn that Desdemona is already pleading his case before Othello.

ACT III, SCENE 2

OVERVIEW AND ANALYSIS

In this brief scene Othello asks Iago to dispatch certain letters to Venice and then meet him at the fortifications. This seven-line scene serves merely to reinforce Othello's dependence on Iago.

ACT III, SCENE 3

OVERVIEW

On the castle grounds Desdemona assures Cassio that she will do everything she can on his behalf with Othello. As Othello and Iago arrive, an embarrassed Cassio hurries off to avoid speaking to Othello. Iago tells Othello that the departing Cassio looked "guilty-like" as he left. Desdemona presses Othello to reconsider stripping Cassio of his title, but Othello seems preoccupied.

After Desdemona and Emilia leave, Iago tells Othello that Cassio's behavior seemed suspicious. Hinting that he knows more than he is saying about Cassio, Iago then manipulates Othello to draw out of him what he "knows." Playing the kind counselor, Iago reminds Othello to be watchful against jealousy ("the green-eyed monster," one of Shakespeare's most famous descriptions).

Iago warns Othello about Desdemona and tells him to "observe her well with Cassio." He also reminds Othello that Desdemona "did deceive her father" when she married him. After planting these seeds of discord, Iago leaves Othello alone. Praising Iago's "exceeding honesty," Othello laments the occurrence of adultery, which he calls the "curse of marriage" committed against "great" men.

When Desdemona and Emilia return, Othello seems distracted and complains of a headache. Desdemona offers to bind his head with a handkerchief, but he pushes it away and it drops unnoticed to the ground as they leave. Recognizing it as an important "token" of Othello and Desdemona's early love, Emilia picks up the handkerchief. Iago, who has been asking her to steal it, snatches it from her.

When Othello reenters he is tormented by jealousy and obsessed with thoughts of Desdemona and Cassio. Threatening Iago with death,

Othello angrily insists that Iago offer proof of Desdemona's infidelity. Iago describes some erotic dreams about Desdemona that he claims to have seen Cassio experience in his sleep. As his final proof Iago says that he saw Cassio wipe his beard with the very handkerchief that was Othello's "first gift" to Desdemona.

In the scene's final moments Othello and Iago kneel as Othello asks Iago (whom he now calls "lieutenant") to murder Cassio within three days. Othello then vows to find some "swift means of death" for "the fair devil," Desdemona.

ANALYSIS

Because the play's entire tragedy turns on this pivotal scene, Shakespeare fills it with some of Iago's most villainous behavior. By already revealing Iago's intentions, Shakespeare adds a layer of dramatic irony to the thoughts and behavior of Iago's victims.

Desdemona's support of Cassio could not be more genuine and heartfelt, and he obviously appreciates the help of this "Bounteous madam." We sense the weight of her closing words that she would "rather die" than stop supporting Cassio.

Iago seizes every opportunity in this scene—from noticing Cassio leaving and suggesting it was a "guilty" departure to railing against the nature of jealousy while he lies to make Othello jealous. Desdemona's determined defense of Cassio to Othello also happens in front of Iago and offers him even more ammunition. As Iago has observed earlier in the play, he will use her "goodness" to weave his web of deceit.

Shakespeare crafts one of his finest scenes of verbal seduction as Iago convinces Othello that his wife has been unfaithful. Iago reveals his "thoughts" slowly, creating anticipation and unnerving Othello, who finally insists: "By heaven, I'll know thy thoughts!" In one of his most cunning moments, Iago returns to Brabantio's warning about Desdemona:

"She did deceive her father." Iago then transfers Brabantio's accusation of witchcraft from Othello to Desdemona.

Racial elements also surface in Iago's rhetoric. He even associates the "unnatural" with loving people of another "complexion"—to Othello's face, no less! Othello seems slowly to crack before our eyes. He begins to question everything about himself, including his age and social standing. The marriage he once cherished now becomes a "curse."

One early critic of *Othello* said the play should have been called *The Tragedy of the Handkerchief.* Despite Emilia's retrieval of the handkerchief and her giving it to Iago, Shakespeare does not in any way implicate her in Iago's destructive intentions. Once she leaves, the Bard again allows us to hear Iago's plotting to plant the handkerchief in Cassio's lodging.

By the time Othello returns to the stage, he is wracked with doubt and suspicion: "I think my wife be honest, and think she is not." Iago claims he is motivated by "foolish honesty and love" to tell Othello everything. His reenactment of Cassio's supposed sexual dream about Desdemona provides one of the play's most disturbing moments. Iago previously referred to jealousy as the "green-eyed monster," and a livid Othello now responds, "I'll tear her all to pieces!" The mention of the handkerchief as Iago's ultimate "proof" of Desdemona's infidelity fills Othello with feelings of vengeance.

In the final act of kneeling between Iago and Othello, Shakespeare unites the two characters in a twisted scene of devotion. As they pledge their allegiance to each other, Iago agrees to murder Cassio, and Othello announces that he will find some "swift means of death" for Desdemona. Iago has finally gotten what he wanted. Othello tells him: "Now art thou my lieutenant." Something sinister attends Iago's final pledge to Othello: "I am your own for ever."

ACT III, SCENE 4

OVERVIEW

At the castle Desdemona asks the clown where Cassio is and the two exchange witticisms. Desdemona then realizes that she has lost the treasured handkerchief Othello gave to her. She tells Emilia she is not worried, however, because Othello is "made of no such baseness/As jealous creatures are."

Othello arrives and demands to see the handkerchief. When Desdemona says she does not have it with her, he describes it as a magic heirloom given to his mother by an Egyptian "charmer." Desdemona tries to hide its loss by changing the subject to Cassio, which sends Othello into a rage, and he leaves.

Iago then enters with Cassio, who asks if Desdemona has convinced Othello to return Cassio to his lieutenancy. Desdemona explains that she must postpone her efforts because Othello seems "altered." Iago acts surprised at the news of Othello's anger and leaves to speak to him. Emilia reiterates previous thoughts about jealousy: "'Tis a monster/Begot upon itself, born on itself."

While Cassio waits for more news, the courtesan Bianca arrives and asks why she has not heard from him. He assures her that everything will return to normal when he is no longer burdened by "leaden thoughts." Cassio then shows Bianca the handkerchief he found in his room; he requests that she copy its design and she agrees. Cassio asks her to leave, as he does not want Othello to see him "womaned."

ANALYSIS

Just as Othello unravels in the previous scene, Desdemona's sense of security begins to fade as this scene progresses. The early discussion between Desdemona and Emilia about jealousy, along with Desdemona's insistence that Othello is free from all jealous feelings, sets up Othello's entrance. He is a study in distrust and suspicion as he demands to see the handkerchief.

Othello behaves more like Iago in this scene: He is manipulative and deceitful and he even makes sexually loaded comments about the "liberal" nature of Desdemona's heart. His speech about the handkerchief's origins seems fabricated solely to make her feel guilty. His words are also prophetic: The handkerchief's loss does lead to disaster ("perdition").

Even though she knows about the handkerchief, Emilia stands silently by watching this horror unfold. "I know not, madam," she tells Desdemona when asked how the handkerchief could have been lost. Is she simply shocked? Because we have no indication that Emilia is involved in her husband's machinations, Shakespeare leaves her behavior open to interpretation.

There would be something humorous about the exchange between Cassio and the courtesan Bianca if it appeared in another play. In this tragedy, though, it follows on the heels of Othello's cruelty to Desdemona about the handkerchief. Shakespeare has us on alert when Cassio asks Bianca to make a copy of the embroidered handkerchief's pattern. What unintended devilry will come from this request?

ACT IV, SCENE 1

OVERVIEW

Iago taunts Othello with crass images of Desdemona "naked . . . in bed" with Cassio. He further torments Othello by bringing up the handkerchief and implying that Cassio has boasted of sleeping with Desdemona. Othello finally faints from distress. Cassio enters but Iago tells him to return after Othello's fit of "epilepsy" has passed. Iago then places Othello within earshot of a conversation between Iago and Cassio. Knowing that Othello will believe they are talking about Desdemona, Iago goads Cassio on to speak about his amorous escapades with Bianca.

Bianca arrives complaining about having to copy the embroidered handkerchief, which she angrily returns to Cassio. After they leave, Iago tells Othello that Cassio has been joking publicly about his affair with Desdemona and has given her handkerchief to a common whore. Othello is enraged, but his words also indicate that he still has some affection for Desdemona.

Iago says he will be Cassio's "undertaker" and suggests that Othello strangle Desdemona in the very bed she has "contaminated." Othello responds, "The justice of it pleases."

Lodovico, one of Desdemona's relatives, arrives from Venice with orders from the Venetian Senate that Othello should return to Venice and leave Cassio in his place in Cyprus. Desdemona, who has entered with

IN A 2007 PRODUCTION AT THE DONMAR
THEATER IN LONDON, OTHELLO (CHIWETEL
EJIOFOR) COLLAPSES IN GRIEF AS IAGO
(EWAN MCGREGOR) LOOKS ON.

Lodovico, begins to speak in Cassio's favor. While Othello reads the letter
he calls her "devil" repeatedly and, in a rage, he strikes her in front of
the others. Lodovico is dumbfounded and asks Iago whether Othello has
gone mad or whether the message from Venice has upset him. Iago replies
that Othello is "much changed."

ANALYSIS

Whereas Roderigo seemed to play the dupe in earlier scenes, Othello
now appears to be putty in Iago's hands. He is open to every one of
Iago's suggestions and believes every foul lie about both Desdemona and
Cassio. His obsessive focus on the handkerchief feeds his association of
Desdemona's supposed infidelity with the lost object. At one point in his

frenzy he exclaims, "Handkerchief—confessions—handkerchief!"

Othello's erratic manner of speech has also changed, and some of his words recall Iago's previous statements. "Goats and monkeys!" Othello cries out at one point—echoing Iago's sexual description in Act III of Desdemona and Cassio as "prime as goats, hot as monkeys." Iago has apparently contaminated Othello's reasoning.

This is indeed a "changed" Othello. How else can we accept his terrible treatment of his wife after Lodovico enters? Through Othello's increasing horror at hearing Iago's lies about Desdemona and Cassio, Shakespeare builds to the explosion, which results in Othello striking his innocent wife. Lodovico's final words indicate that he feels "deceived" by Othello's former goodness; he no longer believes in "the noble Moor."

ACT IV, SCENE 2

OVERVIEW

In a conversation with Othello inside the castle, Emilia defends Desdemona's character as "honest, chaste, and true." She insists that some "wretch" must have put these thoughts of Desdemona's dishonesty into Othello's head. Othello directs her to bring Desdemona to him, but once she leaves he rejects Emilia's heartfelt defense of his wife. He then directs Emilia to wait outside the door, like a "bawd" in a brothel, as he interrogates Desdemona.

As Othello accuses Desdemona of being a "false" wife, she tries in vain to defend her honor. Questioning her in a cruel manner, he accuses her of being a "whore" and a "strumpet." Although Othello weeps at the thought of what his wife has supposedly done and the loss of their love, he refuses to believe her when she protests that she is innocent. Finally he calls Emilia back into the room, pays her for standing guard, and leaves.

Overcome with grief, Desdemona asks Emilia to fetch Iago and then asks him for help with her predicament. As Emilia describes Othello's odious behavior to Iago, she begins to rail against the "eternal villain" and "insinuating rogue" who must have put false thoughts of infidelity in Othello's mind. Emilia insists that some "villainous knave" has "abused" Othello and should be whipped for what he has done. Iago abruptly tells Emilia to shut up and tries to convince Desdemona that the stress of his office is simply wearing on Othello.

As the two women exit, Roderigo enters. He is angry with Iago for avoiding him. Claiming he has been made a fool of, he accuses Iago of doing nothing to aid in his effort to win back Desdemona—despite all the jewels he has given Iago to give to Desdemona. Roderigo threatens to ask for his gifts back, but Iago insists that some hope remains for Roderigo's suit. He informs Roderigo that Cassio is to replace Othello in command at Cyprus and that Othello and Desdemona will soon leave for Mauritania. Iago then convinces Roderigo that they can stop her departure only by "removing" Cassio, by "knocking out his brains," so that Othello will have to stay in Cyprus. They devise a plan to attack Cassio around midnight while he is dining with Bianca.

ANALYSIS

Emilia tries to reason with Othello as this scene opens, but her efforts are all in vain. Othello's treatment of both women as prostitutes in a brothel is tasteless and insulting. Yet, even while he accuses Desdemona of being a whore, he also reveals some flicker of the love he still has left for her, especially in his weeping over what he believes has happened. At one point when Desdemona insists she is not a "whore," Othello shows a brief sign of wavering. "Is't possible?" he asks. Shakespeare wisely leaves some glimmer of Othello's goodness. Otherwise the character would become completely repulsive and there would be no tragedy.

The play's dramatic irony thickens as a desperate Desdemona turns to Iago for help. At this point in the action Iago's assurances that "all things shall be well" have an insidious ring to them. Emilia's increasing anger at the "villain" responsible for poisoning Othello's mind infuriates Iago. Still he reveals no second thoughts, no qualms, about what he has done. Iago is Shakespeare's one villain who is completely devoid of any remorse.

Iago manages to turn Roderigo's righteous anger against the poor fool. We know that Iago has kept Roderigo's jewels for himself and has never given any of them to Desdemona. Would it have made any difference in her nonexistent feelings for Roderigo if he had? Shakespeare conveys a comic undertone in the fool's indignation, but this humor is undercut by Iago's closing plot to enlist Roderigo's aid in killing Cassio.

ACT IV, SCENE 3

OVERVIEW

While walking with Lodovico and some attendants, Othello orders Desdemona to prepare for bed and to dismiss Emilia as well. Left alone the two women prepare Desdemona's bed. Emilia says she has followed Desdemona's orders and dressed the bed with sheets from her wedding night. Desdemona directs Emilia to wrap her in one of the sheets as a shroud if she should die before Emilia.

Desdemona recalls a melancholy song about a willow sung by one of her mother's maids, a woman named Barbary who was deceived in love. As Emilia dresses her for bed, Desdemona sings the sad song about a "scorned" woman. The two women then discuss marital infidelity and whether they would ever be unfaithful to their husbands. Desdemona cannot believe any woman would commit adultery, regardless of the price, but Emilia insists that women are as capable as men of misdeeds in their marriage.

In a previous scene Iago has directed Othello to murder Desdemona in her bed. Othello's directing her at the beginning of this scene to go to bed and to dismiss Emilia creates an immediate sense of discomfort. Despite her discussions of death and sadness, Desdemona remains firm in her love for Othello. Shakespeare uses the melancholic song that Desdemona sings as the scene's musical score, the background music for what is happening on stage. In a comedy a bawdy love song might accompany this scene of domestic preparation, but this play's action is moving in another direction.

The conversation about unfaithfulness in marriage between Desdemona and Emilia reflects both their age and their character. Youthful and pure in spirit, Desdemona still believes that all women are faithful to their husbands. World-weary and coming from another social class, the more experienced Emilia contends that women are just as capable of infidelity as men. In fact she thinks it would be better if men knew that their wives "have sense like them"—that women have the same affections, desires, and weaknesses as men. Emilia concludes that women learn their own misbehavior from the "ills" of their men.

ACT V, SCENE 1

OVERVIEW

Iago and Roderigo meet on a street in Cyprus where, hiding behind a shop front, they are waiting to attack Cassio. As Cassio walks by, Roderigo tries to attack him but fails to hurt him because Cassio is wearing a shirt of mail (a metal chain-link shirt). Cassio then stabs and wounds Roderigo in the leg. Iago jumps out from his hiding place and wounds Cassio in the leg.

Othello—who enters just in time to hear Cassio's cries of "Murder! Murder!"—believes that Iago has kept his promise and killed Cassio.

Othello then runs off to kill Desdemona in her "lust-stained" bed.

Lodovico and Gratiano, another one of Desdemona's Venetian relatives, hear Cassio and Roderigo crying out for help but are hesitant to get involved. Iago returns to the scene with a lantern and pretends that he has suddenly heard the wounded men's cries. Iago stabs Roderigo and kills him and then enlists Lodovico and Gratiano's help with Cassio.

Bianca arrives, but when she bemoans what has happened to Cassio, Iago accuses her of having been part of the plot to hurt Cassio. Iago tells the others: "I do suspect this trash/To be a party in this injury." While Iago continues to point the finger of blame at innocent Bianca, the wounded Cassio is carried off in a chair. When Emilia enters and discovers that Cassio has been hurt, she joins Iago in insulting Bianca as a "strumpet."

ANALYSIS

Iago reveals the full extent of his expedience with others' lives when he remarks that it really does not matter whether Cassio or Roderigo dies. "Every way makes my gain," he observes. Iago admits to having swindled the jewels from Roderigo, and he has no intention of returning them.

Despite Iago's ingenious plotting and his control over many of the characters, he also displays a few signs of worry in this scene. When Cassio's hidden shirt of mail saves him from being killed, Iago contemplates what will happen if Cassio survives. He fears that Cassio's natural reputation ("a daily beauty in his life") may make Iago look "ugly." Iago realizes that, now more than ever, Cassio "must die"—or Othello might reveal Iago's plans to Cassio and thereby expose Iago.

The actor playing Iago must play a character who is also a great actor. Iago's false surprise at Cassio's injury fools everyone else who enters the scene: Lodovico, Gratiano, Bianca, and Emilia. Yet, once all others have left the scene, Iago reveals the importance of what is about to happen: "This is the night/That either makes me or fordoes me quite."

OVERVIEW

Othello enters the bedchamber where Desdemona sleeps and speaks of the "cause" of "justice" he is about to enact. As he kisses his wife and she awakens, Othello bids her to say her final prayers.

Realizing that he plans to murder her, Desdemona insists on her innocence and pleads for her life. She tries to defend Cassio and to tell the truth about the handkerchief, but Othello—thinking that "honest Iago" has killed Cassio—refuses to believe her. Finally he smothers her, though she is not actually dead yet.

AN ENRAGED OTHELLO (NICHOLAS MONU) CONFRONTS DESDEMONA (REBECCA JOHNSON) IN A 2002 PRODUCTION AT LONDON'S COCHRANE THEATER.

Emilia calls at the door. Once Othello lets her enter, she tells him that Cassio is not dead. Hearing her mistress's moans, Emilia then discovers Desdemona in the throes of death. Desdemona, remaining faithful to Othello, refuses to name him as her murderer. Then she dies.

At first Othello denies having killed Desdemona, but then he admits what he has done. Once Othello reveals that it was Iago who informed him of Desdemona's infidelity, Emilia realizes what her husband has done. Emilia cries "Murder," bringing Iago, Montano, and Gratiano racing into the room.

When Emilia explains the truth about the handkerchief, Othello tries to kill Iago but only wounds him. As Iago flees, he fatally stabs Emilia; she dies repeating some of the "Willow" song that was previously sung by Desdemona. Lodovico, Montano, and some officers return with Iago as their prisoner and Cassio (still recuperating in a chair). Letters found on Roderigo's body reveal Iago's involvement in the plot and clear Cassio of any wrongdoing.

Now aware that he was mistaken all along about Desdemona, Othello stabs himself and falls on the bed next to Desdemona. As the play ends Lodovico directs Cassio to "torture" the "hellish villain" Iago.

ANALYSIS

In his final murderous moments, Othello still exhibits some love for Desdemona. Although he is compelled to kiss her, his overstimulated sense of doling out justice for his wife's infidelity drives his actions. Even in death Desdemona remains strong, insisting on her innocence, trying to reason with her enraged husband, and refusing to blame him for murdering her. She is one of Shakespeare's purist creations. Emilia calls her "the sweetest innocent."

Iago's treacherous influence on Othello seems apparent when Othello at first lies to Emilia about Desdemona's death. Emilia's loyalty to Desdemona shines in this scene, as does her indignation over what Iago has done. The name "villain" is finally and properly assigned to Iago, and Lodovico also refers to him as "this slave."

It's an undeniably busy scene, with stabbings that are both wounding and fatal, quick entrances and exits, and almost all the major characters on stage. Othello's final description of himself as "one that loved not wisely, but too well" has become one of the play's most quoted lines. In what seems like a desperate attempt to reinstate his reputation, Othello's final words describe one of his military conquests. Cassio, offering one small tribute to the dying Othello, says that the general was "great of heart."

LIST OF CHARACTERS

Othello, the Moor of Venice and protagonist of the play

Iago, Othello's ensign, sometimes referred to as his "ancient"

Desdemona, a Venetian lady and Othello's wife

Emilia, Iago's wife and attendant to Desdemona

Cassio, Othello's lieutenant

Roderigo, a Venetian gentleman

Brabantio, Desdemona's father and a member of the Venetian Senate

Duke of Venice

Bianca, a courtesan, in love with Cassio

Montano, the governor of Cyprus

Gratiano, a Venetian nobleman and Brabantio's brother

Lodovico, a Venetian nobleman and relative to Brabantio

The clown, a comic servant to Othello and Desdemona

Herald, officers, servants, attendants, messengers, musicians, torchbearers

ANALYSIS OF MAJOR CHARACTERS

OTHELLO

Shakespeare crafted one of his most complex tragic heroes in Othello. The brave, self-assured general we meet at the beginning of the play seems to bear little resemblance to the tortured, ruined man who has lost everything dear to him at the end. As the play progresses we watch the accomplished general slowly unravel before our eyes.

Even though we first hear of the title character through the resentful voice of Iago, Othello manages to dominate the stage upon his entrance. Announcing his own "royal" lineage, Othello immediately presents a confident figure. "I fetch my life and being/From men of royal siege," he proudly tells Iago. Othello is also a respected military leader held in high esteem by the Venetian Senate. In both character and reputation, Othello seems like a decisive man who is bound for further greatness.

Othello's command of the scene when Brabantio brings charges against him shows that he has a level head in a potentially dangerous situation. His reputation precedes him, and we can sense that the duke's sympathies lie first with Othello. Even though Othello calls himself "rude" in speech, he speaks quite eloquently when describing both his love for Desdemona and his own life story. He admits to becoming a military man early in his childhood. How can we not admire this man of action who has survived slavery and so many near-death dangers?

On the other hand Othello possesses a certain naïve and trusting attitude toward others. By introducing Iago before Othello, Shakespeare establishes Iago's treacherous character from the very beginning. Othello's repeated use of the word *honest* to describe Iago seems to betray a certain lack of perception. Is it also a clue to Othello's sudden mistrust of his young, faithful wife that he has so obviously misjudged Iago? Othello is so sure of Iago's loyalty, and so sure in the beginning of Desdemona's love, that little room exists in his mind for life's grayer and less obvious areas.

Othello appears to wear his heart on his sleeve, especially concerning Desdemona. In his first speech he announces his love for her in the same breath as he refers to his prized freedom. Yet Brabantio's warning about his daughter has a certain sting: How well does Othello really know Desdemona? Pure of heart and innocent, she is much younger than Othello and has been easily impressed by tales of his dangerous life. His character seems to need this unconditional adulation and will not allow for any threat to it. Does his attitude reflect a secure personality?

One of the sources of Othello's complexity is his place as an outsider in Venetian society. As an African Moor, Othello—although he is respected for his military deeds—is also mistrusted for his ethnicity. Throughout the play Iago, Roderigo, and Brabantio openly insult Othello's race. Brabantio feels no qualms about accusing Othello of witchcraft in front of the Senate. We hear frequently about his being "black" (just as Othello comments on Desdemona's whiteness). On stage and in films Othello has been played by both white and black actors, from the white British actor Laurence Olivier to Laurence Fishburne, the first black actor to play the role on film.

The play's dual setting also reflects on Othello's character and behavior. Othello has been in Venice, a city of high culture, for only a few months. As he observes early in the play, he is more accustomed to the "tented field" of military battles. Is the more impulsive Othello we encounter in

the colony of Cyprus closer to his true personality?

Othello's militaristic personality, his naïveté, and his ethnic and racial place as an outsider set him up for Iago's manipulation. Yet it is the nature of his jealousy that has drawn the most attention over the centuries. Once Othello allows Iago's accusations to influence him, his personality becomes obsessive. The love he has so strongly proclaimed for Desdemona unravels almost immediately in his mind, and he begins to accept and to look for every possibility of his wife's infidelity. Othello's jealousy is so strong that it moves him to madness.

Othello places so much value on the handkerchief that his wife supposedly gave Cassio that he seems to transfer his affection from his wife to an object. The handkerchief, a "pledge of love" he gave to Desdemona, also carries the weight of Othello's heritage. As he points out in the final scene, it was "an antique token" that his father gave to his mother.

Despite all of Othello's flaws, one of the main sources for the play's overwhelming tragedy is that, even to the end, he exhibits signs of his love for his wife. His inner conflict is so strong that at one point in the play he faints. However, as the final scene reveals, Othello's love for Desdemona is no match for the overblown sense of "justice" that he repeatedly refers to as his "cause." The idealistic soldier we meet earlier in the play now places ideals above people.

Ultimately Othello chooses a military solution to his dilemma. First he kills the innocent and faithful wife whom he perceives as the enemy, and then, realizing the mistake he has made, he kills himself. Even as he stabs himself, Othello describes killing an enemy—"a malignant and a turbaned Turk"—on the battlefield. The once proud military man falls, dying, onto his marriage bed.

IAGO

The villain of *Othello*, Iago commands the stage from his first appearance. Even when he is not on stage, his haunting figure dominates the play. It is certainly no accident that Shakespeare chose to introduce the vengeful Iago before Othello. In *King Lear* a number of characters are evil, but Shakespeare concentrates all of *Othello*'s evil in the figure of Iago. In this sense Shakespeare lends a disturbing importance to his villainous creation, making Iago one of the most famous and most desirable dramatic roles in history.

Iago may also have his origins in the "Vice character" from the morality plays of the Middle Ages. Vice characters usually tempt others into misbehaving and then take pleasure in the consequences suffered by these people who were once good. Whereas the Vice characters were often comic, closer to Shakespeare's Falstaff, Iago remains evil throughout *Othello*. Iago's speech in Act I, in which he mocks the value of "virtue," indicates his immoral character and his association with the Vice figure.

On the surface Iago's motivation seems apparent. As the play opens he immediately defines himself as a spiteful character. He has lost the lieutenancy to Cassio and resents being reduced to Othello's "ancient" (or ensign). Iago's early comments indicate that he believes he has been swindled out of the position he deserves and is now trapped in a lower social position. In his own way Iago—like Othello—views himself as an outsider in the cultured society of Venice.

In his first scene Iago also quickly establishes the deceptive nature of his personality. Insisting that his actions will never reveal his intentions, he tells Roderigo, "I am not what I am." Unlike Othello, Iago refuses to wear his heart upon his sleeve. Once alone on stage, Iago insults his master, Othello: "I do hate him as I do hell-pains." In his first encounter with Othello, however, he is pledging his love and loyalty to the general. Iago's hatred is static, unwavering, for he exposes it in the beginning and he never changes. Even in his final scene he refuses to "speak word" about what he has done, remaining true only to his own twisted sense of values.

Iago is a master of manipulation, another trait that Shakespeare establishes early in the play. He goads the foolish Roderigo, a gentleman of higher social position, into causing a ruckus to rouse Desdemona's father. Throughout the play Iago cleverly uses Roderigo for his own purposes. Iago works his way into Othello's confidence and then slowly and carefully persuades him that Desdemona has been unfaithful with Cassio. He has no qualms about killing others to get what he wants.

Watching Iago's villainy working on Othello's peace of mind is one of *Othello*'s most enjoyable aspects, because we know the character is a wicked mastermind. In Act III, when Iago's lies begin to affect Othello, Iago gloats: "The Moor already changes with my poison." In every scene—with every sinister word—Iago holds our undivided attention.

Iago is also a master of rhetoric who knows the sheer power of words and readily employs them to his own advantage. Like a chameleon changing hue to blend into its environment, he alters his words to fit the situation at hand—convincing Roderigo that he has a chance with Desdemona or persuading Othello that Desdemona is untrue. Iago constructs his own reasons for his actions, reasons that often have no basis in reality. At different times he makes ridiculous claims to justify his own hatred—for example, claiming that Othello has slept with Emilia (Iago's wife). As he openly admits, Iago uses these fabrications to feed his "revenge." Iago bluntly states his intention: to play on Othello's "peace and quiet/Even to madness."

In addition Iago's character reveals little respect for women. In his initial scene with Desdemona and Emilia, he mocks women and paints a deceitful portrait of them in general. While his words seem to be in jest, they also serve as a disturbing warning of his disregard for women. Iago goads Othello on in killing Desdemona. He uses Emilia in his plot to destroy Othello and in the final scene kills his wife when she reveals the crimes he has committed.

Some of the world's finest actors have played Iago on stage and in film, including Christopher Plummer, Ian McKellen, Kenneth Branagh, and Ewan McGregor. The character of Iago has served as the inspiration for a number of evil counselors who work toward the destruction of their masters, such as Gríma Wormtongue in J.R.R. Tolkien's *The Lord of the Rings*.

DESDEMONA

The young bride of Othello, Desdemona, is central to the main conflict of the play. In all of her scenes Desdemona acts out of the kindness of her heart with every character that surrounds her. She is both the object of her husband's love and the victim of his jealousy. More importantly she is a character who never wavers in her love for her husband or in defense of her reputation. Desdemona may seem weak or secondary, but her goodness becomes strength in a tragedy that focuses on the power struggle between good and evil.

Like Juliet in *Romeo and Juliet* and Jessica in *The Merchant of Venice,* Desdemona defies her father to pursue her romantic interest. In her first appearance she openly declares her love for Othello and informs her father that her "duty" now belongs to her new husband. Her father, Brabantio, reflecting the prejudiced views of Venetian society, says that her love for Othello is "against all rules of nature," but his objections do not stop her.

Modern audiences may also notice another streak of defiance in Desdemona, who openly announces that she "did love the Moor to live with him." Desdemona is surprisingly open about her sensuality. There is nothing shy or retiring about this young woman! She even asks the duke if she may accompany Othello on his military mission to Cyprus. The world Desdemona encounters in Cyprus is very different from the wealthy, cultured one she leaves behind in Venice.

At one point in the play Cassio refers to Desdemona as "our great captain's captain." Desdemona also quickly exchanges witty remarks with Iago in her first encounter with him. She seems capable of holding her own with anyone. Her support for Cassio indicates her strong sense of loyalty. She readily takes up his case and speaks on his behalf: Out of the goodness of her heart she pleads with Othello to reinstate Cassio after he is dismissed for fighting.

On the other hand Desdemona also displays signs of her youth and naïveté. In her conversation with Emilia about women and infidelity,

Desdemona cannot accept the idea that women can be unfaithful to their husbands. "I do not think there is any such woman," she says to Emilia. Desdemona also tells Emilia that she believes Othello does not possess a jealous nature: "I think the sun where he was born/Drew all such humors from him." Yet, the Othello we encounter as the play progresses is mad with jealousy. How well does Desdemona really know her husband?

Desdemona's love for her husband is her strongest motivation. She proclaims her love for Othello to the very end—even in the last scene in which he kills her. Her final words do not point the finger at Othello, who has recently smothered her. Instead she claims that her killer was "Nobody—I myself" and dies. Is this foolishness or fidelity? Over the centuries various actors have played Desdemona in a number of ways, from innocent and girlish to strong and feisty.

The "divine" Desdemona, as Cassio refers to her, continues to fascinate and challenge the actors who play her.

EMILIA

Emilia, Iago's wife, provides the voice of reason in *Othello*—although her wisest comments come late in the play. She also offers the strongest defense of Desdemona's character, but her words to Othello fall on deaf ears. Throughout many of her scenes Emilia reveals wisdom and understanding that Shakespeare grants to no other character in this tragedy.

Emilia's loyalties are somewhat divided between Iago and Desdemona. Until she realizes what her husband has done, Emilia remains loyal to Iago throughout much of the tragedy. She endures his snide remarks about wives and women in general and is clever enough to offer her own responses. When she finds Desdemona's lost handkerchief, she gives it to Iago (who has frequently asked for it). Yet she also worries that its loss will upset Desdemona and tries to compel Iago to return it to her.

Emilia's comments on jealousy in Act III, Scene 4 accurately describe the terrible change in Othello's character. She observes how jealousy feeds on itself and becomes its own cause. "'Tis a monster/Begot upon itself, born on itself," she tells Desdemona. Shakespeare appears to be using Emilia to reflect one of the play's basic themes. When Othello confronts Emilia about his wife's infidelity, she says that she would "lay down" her soul that Desdemona is "honest, chaste, and true."

Emilia's more worldly character also serves as a contrast to Desdemona's innocence. Emilia's speech about women being just as capable of disloyalty as men seems quite modern and enlightened for Shakespeare's time. She says, "Let husbands know/Their wives have sense like them." Desdemona cannot accept the thought that women can also be unfaithful, but the more experienced Emilia insists that women have the same "affections" and "desires" as men.

In the tragedy's final scene, Shakespeare uses Emilia's voice to reveal the sad truth to Othello. Realizing that Othello has killed her "sweet mistress," Emilia at first cannot believe what Iago has done to cause this tragedy. Overcoming her duty to her husband, Emilia insists that Iago has lied to Othello about Desdemona's unfaithfulness. Emilia also displays no sign of weakness or fear toward Othello or any other man in the play. "I care not for thy sword," she tells him once she exposes what he has done.

Shakespeare also uses Emilia to confront Iago and to expose him at the end. She refuses to listen to her husband when he tells her not to speak. After she says she will not let "heaven and men and devils" stop her from telling the truth about her husband's villainous lies, Iago kills her for being honest. In more modern productions Emilia's character has received more force and attention.

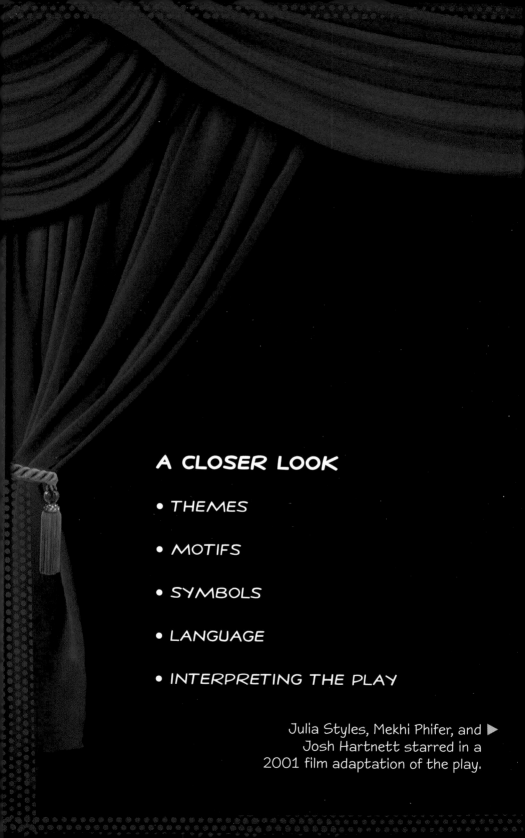

A CLOSER LOOK

- THEMES

- MOTIFS

- SYMBOLS

- LANGUAGE

- INTERPRETING THE PLAY

Julia Styles, Mekhi Phifer, and ▶
Josh Hartnett starred in a
2001 film adaptation of the play.

BHIFER HARTNETT STILES

"O"

TRUST.
SEDUCTION.
BETRAYAL.

EVERYTHING COMES FULL CIRCLE

66929 **Chapter Three** 66929

CHAPTER THREE

A Closer Look

THEMES

THE DIFFERENCE BETWEEN APPEARANCE AND REALITY

One of Shakespeare's major themes throughout most of his work is also the main theme and central conflict of *Othello:* the difference between appearance and reality. The play explores the terrible tragedy that results when a basically good character can no longer discern the difference between what actually is and what only seems to be. Othello is so strongly manipulated by Iago into believing that Desdemona has been unfaithful that he stops believing in his wife.

The flaws in Othello's character worsen his tendency to believe what he hears over what he knows. Although it may appear that Desdemona has been untrue—thanks in great part to Iago's lies—Othello fails to question the evidence. Instead he accepts the appearance of infidelity as the truth. His obsession with the appearance of unfaithfulness leads Othello into madness and revenge.

In an ironic twist on the theme, Othello believes in his wicked ensign, Iago, more than he believes in his wife. Iago offers Othello the appearance of support and loyalty, yet in reality he works constantly to bring down Othello. Iago believes he can rely on Othello to trust him because—as he says—Othello has "a free and open nature/That thinks men honest that but seem to be so."

To make matters worse Othello begins to view his wife's goodness as an act, as if she only appears to be innocent. Believing Iago's lies, Othello accuses the most "honest" person in his life—his wife—of being "false," yet he repeatedly refers to Iago as "honest."

Shakespeare emphasizes the force of this theme by allowing his audience to know the truth and to see the difference between appearance and reality. At every turn we hear Iago's true intentions: We know that his words are lies and that his loyalty to Othello is only an act. While the characters become caught in a dangerous web, the audience always knows the truth. In this way the Bard reinforces his major theme, along with the tragedy of what happens.

"T'IS NEITHER HERE NOR THERE."

THE DESTRUCTIVE NATURE OF JEALOUSY

Although it would be simplistic to describe *Othello* as simply a play about jealousy, Othello's overwhelming jealousy drives much of the play's action. Shakespeare illustrates the tragic consequences of allowing jealousy to rule one's behavior. In *Othello*, jealousy serves as a destructive power that destroys real love and can leave a jealous person alone and ruined.

Emilia's comments on jealousy in Act III indicate the play's major premise. People are jealous not so much for any specific "cause" but simply because they are jealous. Jealousy is a part of human nature: When it takes over, a person loses all sense of reason. Emilia's comment that jealousy is a monster "born on itself" applies to both Iago and Othello. Iago is driven by his jealousy for Cassio, who has received the lieutenant position that Iago feels he deserved. Othello's jealousy feeds on itself throughout the play and eventually drives him to madness and murder.

In an ironic twist it is Iago who first warns Othello about jealousy. "It is the green-eyed monster," he tells Othello while he plants the seeds of jealousy in the general's open mind. Iago knows the effect of jealousy and that "Trifles light as air" can be proof enough to a jealous mind. Using this knowledge he masterminds the play's tragic events.

Shakespeare also reinforces the notion that jealousy is a trait mostly hidden inside a person. Othello's jealous nature seems to escape most of the characters, except, of course, for Iago, who plays on it. When Emilia asks Desdemona if Othello is jealous, Desdemona responds that it is not in his nature. Yet, throughout much of the play, Othello is obsessed with the thought that Cassio has slept with Desdemona.

Does awareness of age also contribute to jealousy—especially when one person is much older than the other? The age difference between Othello and Desdemona may also play a factor in his jealousy. Othello points out in Act III that he has "declined/Into the vale of years," meaning he has become older. In his final speech Othello defends himself against charges of simply being jealous. He insists he was not "easily jealous" and claims instead that he "loved not wisely, but too well."

THE CONFLICT BETWEEN PASSION AND REASON

One of the most universal themes appearing in *Othello* is the conflict between passion and reason. Most people can relate to the strong feelings exhibited by the main characters: love, jealousy, envy, and hate. In Elizabethan times people were supposed to maintain a balance between their feelings and their intellect. Passions should be controlled by a person's reason. In *Othello* Shakespeare illustrates what happens when passion get the better of his characters.

Early in the play, when Iago tries to stop Roderigo from drowning himself, he tells him that "we have reason" to control our emotions and our lust. Iago suggests that instead of killing himself Roderigo should use his rational mind to overcome his strong desires for Desdemona. Iago's arguments also lead to his racist accusations that "Moors" are "changeable in their wills," implying that North African people are less guided by their reason. Iago uses his own warped reasoning to convince Roderigo to continue in his passionate and ridiculous pursuit of Desdemona.

Shakespeare also poses the question: Has their passion for one another driven Othello and Desdemona to marry too soon? We hear of their wide age difference and their different cultural backgrounds. Desdemona admits that she knows of no signs of jealousy in Othello, whereas Othello readily believes his young wife can be unfaithful. His rational mind seems not to be working when he actually believes his wife has been with Cassio "a thousand times." How well do the two characters really know each other? Are they blinded by their passion?

Tying in with the theme of jealousy, Iago openly states that he wants to "put the Moor/At least into a jealousy so strong/That judgment cannot cure." Through his lies Iago hopes that Othello's judgment will be unable to overcome his jealousy. Othello struggles with his strong and irrational feelings until his reason gives way to his misguided passion. When Desdemona finally realizes that Othello intends to murder her, she observes, "Some bloody passion shakes your very frame." Throughout the play she tries in vain to reason with her husband, but her words cannot overcome his passions.

MOTIFS

Throughout *Othello* Shakespeare repeatedly uses monster imagery to reinforce irrational and inhuman behavior. Is Iago simply a monster who destroys everything around him? Does Othello turn into a monster when his jealousy drives him to kill his innocent young wife? Through the recurring use of monster images, Shakespeare's play makes a case for the monster that may reside in even the purest heart.

At the end of his soliloquy in Act I, Scene 3, Iago describes his destructive plotting as a "monstrous birth" that he has brought into the world. His evil mind has given birth to a terrible idea that he will nurture and grow. While falsely counseling Othello not to become jealous, Iago

"ON HORROR'S HEAD HORRORS ACCUMULATE."

refers to jealousy as "the green-eyed monster." When Iago describes Cassio's dream of having slept with Desdemona, Othello cries out in his anguish: "O monstrous! monstrous!"

Later in the play Emilia describes jealousy as "a monster/Begot upon itself, born on itself." Desdemona responds, "Heaven keep that monster from Othello's mind!" Othello's description of his determination to kill Desdemona as a "strong conception" he groans with also plays on the birthing image. In this way Shakespeare ties together two motifs: the monster and the image of its birth, brought on by itself. These comments repeat Iago's original description of his evil plot as a birth.

Iago also plays on the fact that, in Elizabethan times, a man whose wife had been unfaithful was often called "a cuckold." Cuckolds were usually depicted as men with horns, another type of monster or devil. Othello refers to a cuckold as "a horned man . . . a monster and a beast." In the final scene Emilia refers to Othello as "a devil" and Montano calls Othello's murder of Desdemona a "monstrous act."

Shakespeare employs many military motifs in this play about a general who loses everything. Othello's first description of himself is filled with images of "battles, sieges, [and] fortunes." He says that Desdemona loves him for the "dangers" he has experienced in his military life. At one point in the play Cassio speaks highly of Desdemona's reputation and calls her "our great captain's captain." He uses the military title to refer to the power he believes she has over Othello, a military hero.

Through the repetition of these military images, Shakespeare sets up a conflict between the cultured person and the military person. Early in the play Othello apologizes to the Venetian Senate because he is "Rude" in speech. Instead, he claims he is better suited to "the tented field," referring to the scene of military battles. When the clown asks the musicians to stop playing, he informs them that "to hear music the general does not greatly care." Coming from the highly cultured city-state of Venice, Iago refers to Cyprus as "this warlike isle."

Once Othello begins to doubt Desdemona and lose his mind, he also laments the loss of his military career. In a speech filled with military images, Othello cries:

> FAREWELL THE PLUMÈD TROOP, AND THE BIG WARS
> THAT MAKE AMBITION VIRTUE! O FAREWELL!
> FAREWELL THE NEIGHING STEED AND THE SHRILL TRUMP,
> THE SPIRIT-STIRRING DRUM, TH' EAR-PIERCING FIFE,
> THE ROYAL BANNER, AND ALL QUALITY,
> PRIDE, POMP, AND CIRCUMSTANCE OF GLORIOUS WAR!

The motif of kneeling provides another of the play's most disturbing images. Although we never see a marriage scene between Othello and Desdemona, Othello kneels down with Iago at one point to take "a sacred vow." Kneeling beside Othello, Iago pledges his "wit, hands, heart/To wronged Othello's service." While they are kneeling in this scene that resembles a warped marriage vow, Othello asks Iago to kill Cassio. Othello then commits himself to murdering Desdemona.

Shakespeare repeats the image of kneeling when Desdemona kneels before Othello to ask him to clarify his accusations: "Upon my knees, what doth your speech import?" While kneeling, she pledges her allegiance to her husband as his "true and loyal wife." Desdemona later kneels again, this time before Iago, to ask for his help. "Here I kneel," she tells him as she professes her innocence to the very person who has been her undoing. The parallels to the earlier scene of Othello and Iago kneeling together are unmistakable.

In no other play by Shakespeare does an object carry as much symbolic weight as the handkerchief in *Othello*. Throughout the play it has a number of symbolic purposes. The handkerchief immediately functions as a symbol of early love between Othello and Desdemona. It is at

IAGO (TIM MCINNERNY) SNATCHES THE HANDKERCHIEF FROM EMILIA (LORRAINE BURROUGHS) IN A PRODUCTION AT SHAKESPEARE'S GLOBE THEATER, LONDON, 2007.

first carelessly dropped by Othello when Desdemona offers him the handkerchief to bind his forehead because of a headache. He says he refuses it because it is "too little," and it falls unnoticed to the ground. We learn from Emilia, who finds it, that the handkerchief was Desdemona's "first remembrance"—her first gift—from Othello.

When Emilia gives the handkerchief to Iago, who has repeatedly asked her for it, the object becomes woven into his evil plan. Iago reveals he will intentionally "lose" the object in Cassio's lodgings, so that Cassio can find it there. Symbolically, Iago has transferred Desdemona's affection for Othello to Cassio.

Othello goes into a rage when Iago accurately describes the strawberry pattern on the handkerchief and says he saw Cassio wipe his beard with it. At this point in the play the handkerchief becomes Othello's final proof, a symbol of Desdemona's infidelity (strawberries are shaped somewhat like hearts).

To Othello the handkerchief also serves as a symbol of his heritage. When he confronts Desdemona about its location, he tells the story of its origin. Othello says an Egyptian woman, "a charmer" who could "read/ The thoughts of people," gave the handkerchief to his mother. We hear about the handkerchief's power to control affections between Othello's mother and father—and the danger of its loss. Losing it, Othello tells Desdemona, leads to disaster.

The handkerchief also comes to represent Othello's obsessive jealousy. He clings to the mistaken thought that his wife has given this token of his love and heritage to another man, Cassio. When he confronts Desdemona, he keeps repeating: "The handkerchief! . . . The handkerchief!" Even in the final scene, when Desdemona denies having ever given it to Cassio, Othello accuses her of lying. Ultimately the handkerchief becomes a symbol of truth when Emilia tells Othello that she gave it to Iago who had "begged" her to steal it. The former proof of his wife's unfaithfulness now becomes the proof of Iago's villainy.

Throughout *Othello*, Shakespeare uses the color black to represent evil and to reflect on Othello's place as a social outsider. Insults to Othello's race should not be confused with all uses of the color black. Although Othello is a North African, he receives only respect and admiration from the Venetian Senate, whose members side with him against Brabantio and support him as their military general. As the duke tells Brabantio: "Your son-in-law is far more fair than black." In this instance, the word *fair* implies true and virtuous, whereas the term *black*—though a pun on Othello's race—symbolizes a wicked or malevolent personality.

Iago, Roderigo, and Brabantio insult Othello by referring disparagingly to his "blackness." Throughout the play Iago refers to Othello only as "the Moor," emphasizing his awareness of Othello's race. When speaking about the general with Cassio, Iago calls him "black Othello." When he tells Brabantio of Desdemona's elopement with Othello, Iago refers to Othello as "an old black ram" and Desdemona as a "white ewe."

Because a ram also has horns, Iago crafts an association between the black ram and the horned image of the devil. The blending of the color black and devil imagery occurs again in Act II, Scene 1, when Iago tells Roderigo that Desdemona will tire of looking at Othello: ". . . what delight shall she have to look on the devil?" In Act II, Scene 3, Iago repeats this connection between the color black and the devil when he comments on devils encouraging people to commit "the blackest sins."

Shakespeare sets up a recurring contrast between black and white. Othello points out Desdemona's whiteness when he watches her sleeping before he smothers her to death. He says that her skin is "whiter . . . than snow" and "smooth as . . . alabaster." When Othello admits to Emilia that he has killed Desdemona, she responds: "O, the more angel she,/And you the blacker devil."

Although Othello refers to his own blackness ("I am black") at different points in the play, he also uses the color negatively to describe "black vengeance" when he hears about the handkerchief and is moved to rage. The symbolically negative use of the color black is not specific to *Othello*. Shakespeare uses colors throughout his plays and poems in a highly imaginative way.

LANGUAGE

Although Othello has some powerful speeches, including his inspiring descriptions of his youthful military life and his early declarations of love for Desdemona, Shakespeare reserves the play's most impressive language for Iago. Because Iago is a master of rhetoric, he is particularly adroit at using words for his own purposes. Note that Shakespeare has Iago speak in prose when he is manipulating Roderigo and verse when conniving with Othello.

Many of the most quoted lines from *Othello* belong to Iago; some of his observations have become proverbial in their usage. Centuries after it was invented, his remark about "the green-eyed monster" is still a recognizable metaphor for jealousy. In another enduring metaphor, Iago warns, "Our bodies are our gardens, to the which our wills are gardeners. . . ." In a frequently quoted observation, Iago comments on the price of losing one's good reputation: "Who steals my purse steals trash . . ./But he that filches from me my good name/Robs me of that which not enriches him/And makes me poor indeed." This extended metaphor also carries a great deal of irony—the most notorious thief in the play is Iago!

As rhetoric Iago's arguments may make sense on one level—but a closer look reveals his twisted reasoning. Shakespeare fills Iago's speeches, especially his soliloquies, with bold and suggestive imagery that illustrates his warped logic. Iago's soliloquy at the end of Act II, Scene 1 offers a fine example:

> THAT CASSIO LOVES HER, I DO WELL BELIEVE'T;
> THAT SHE LOVES HIM, 'TIS APT AND OF GREAT CREDIT.
> THE MOOR, HOWBEIT THAT I ENDURE HIM NOT,
> IS OF A CONSTANT, LOVING, NOBLE NATURE,
> AND I DARE THINK HE'LL PROVE TO DESDEMONA
> A MOST DEAR HUSBAND. NOW I DO LOVE HER TOO;
> NOT OUT OF ABSOLUTE LUST, THOUGH PERADVENTURE
> I STAND ACCOUNTANT FOR AS GREAT A SIN,
> BUT PARTLY LED TO DIET MY REVENGE,
> FOR THAT I DO SUSPECT THE LUSTY MOOR
> HATH LEAPED INTO MY SEAT; THE THOUGHT WHEREOF
> DOTH, LIKE A POISONOUS MINERAL, GNAW MY INWARDS;
> AND NOTHING CAN OR SHALL CONTENT MY SOUL
> TILL I AM EVENED WITH HIM, WIFE FOR WIFE. . . .

Iago begins this speech by stating three simple facts: Cassio loves Desdemona, Desdemona loves him back in an acceptable and admirable fashion, and Othello has a true and loyal nature. Iago repeats his view of Othello's loyalty by commenting that the Moor will make a "most dear husband" to Desdemona. A pun on "dear" occurs in its double meaning of (1) a loving husband, and (2) an expensive one. If Iago's plotting succeeds it will, indeed, cost Desdemona her husband—an expensive price to pay.

Notice also Iago's use of words associated with money: *credit, dear, accountant*. Resentful and envious, he is always keeping score and thinking in monetary terms. His repeated use of the word *purse* throughout the play reinforces his mercantile attitudes.

Because Iago also needs a motivation, he invents one: Midway through the speech he decides that he also loves Desdemona. Yet it is not his "lust" for Desdemona that defines his sin but his desire to use her in his vengeful plot—to feed ("diet") his revenge, as he says. Iago then claims that "lusty" Othello "Hath leapt into my seat." The metaphoric use of the word *seat* holds a number of meanings here, including Iago's rightful "place" as a husband with Emilia and the saddle on a horse. In his use of sexual imagery, Iago plays again on the notion of Othello as the "black ram" who has mounted the "white ewe." Iago fabricates a new motivation for hating Othello: The Moor has slept with Emilia.

Iago employs one of many similes when he states that the thought of Othello stealing his "place" with Emilia eats away at his innards "like a poisonous mineral." Shakespeare loves to repeat his imagery, especially within each play. Iago's simile recalls Brabantio's earlier accusation that Othello had used "drugs or minerals" to seduce Desdemona. Shakespeare imparts a certain irony to the final words of his master rhetorician. Iago states: "From this time forth I never will speak word."

INTERPRETING THE PLAY

PLAYING OTHELLO IN BLACK AND WHITE

Discussions of race in *Othello* must be placed into historical context. As Britain became more involved in the slave trade in the seventeenth century, the image of a black hero proved increasingly problematic in productions. At times white actors in England played Othello as a light-skinned Moor to avoid any potential offensiveness to white audiences.

Many nineteenth-century scholars, including the Romantic poets Samuel Taylor Coleridge and Charles Lamb, argued about the validity of Othello's "blackness." Because these writers and directors were white in a time of segregated societies, they could not accept the thought of a truly "black" Shakespearean hero.

In England the tendency to play Othello as a white man (and, thus, by a white actor) was finally broken in 1930 when the African-American singer Paul Robeson played Othello in London. A black actor did not play Othello on stage in the Southern United States until 1979—and when he kissed Desdemona, audiences gasped and wrote hate letters.

Such revered African-American actors as James Earl Jones and Laurence Fishburne have lent their enormous talents to the role of Othello. With varying success, white actors such as Laurence Olivier and Orson Welles have played Othello in dark makeup. In 1997 the British-born actor Patrick Stewart played a white Othello in an all-black production, turning the play's racial imbalance on its head.

Contemporary playwrights have addressed the racial aspect from more political perspectives. For example, in Charles Marowitz's *An Othello* (1974), Iago is recast as a black radical questioning Othello's real motives. At the end of the play, Iago asks Othello: "Are you going to be a tool of white audiences just to give them a catharsis?" In *Harlem Duet* (1998), Canadian playwright Djanet Sears moves the action of Othello to Harlem in the nineteenth and twentieth centuries and focuses on the interracial marriage between Othello and Desdemona. Sears has referred to her play as "a rhapsodic blues tragedy."

A VILLAIN'S POINT OF VIEW

Shakespeare's inventive use of point of view in *Othello* brings the audience and reader closer to the events of this tragedy than to any other. By introducing us first to Iago and by immediately establishing Iago's hatred for Othello, Shakespeare creates a second layer of perspective that he adroitly maintains throughout the play. The establishment of Iago as the first and strongest voice in *Othello* also adds an element of irony to many of the play's events.

In *Othello* it is the self-proclaimed villain who repeatedly takes us into his confidence. In this sense Shakespeare cleverly brings us closest to Iago: We may sympathize with the other characters, but a part of us watches from Iago's viewpoint. Through Iago Shakespeare appears to hold a mirror up to his audience. It may be easier to hate or feel disgust for Iago, but what part of ourselves do we see reflected in his odious behavior? This focused point of view brings us closer to the often destructive consequences of feelings of envy and resentment.

Iago's words of intent regarding his plotting to destroy Othello keep us on the lookout for every character, event, or object that might feed into his malicious scheme. Therefore, Shakespeare adds a strong sense of dramatic irony to many events that seem innocuous. We cringe when Othello repeatedly calls Iago "honest," or when Cassio offers strong words of praise for Desdemona, or when a distraught Desdemona asks Iago for help. We know what the characters do not know: that Iago will use these good intentions to his own advantage, the essence of dramatic irony.

ATTITUDES TOWARD WOMEN IN OTHELLO

Perceptions of the two main women in *Othello*, Desdemona and Emilia, have altered as attitudes toward women have changed. For many centuries the two women were played mostly as victims; at times their roles were minimized and their lines deleted. Upon closer inspection, many of the lines Shakespeare wrote reveal two characters who often transcend the subordinate roles assigned to women in Elizabethan times.

Desdemona's loyalty to Othello and her love for her older husband drive her to remain faithful to him even as he becomes abusive. To modern audiences, this fealty may seem self-defeating and dangerous. Women had certain responsibilities to their husbands in Shakespeare's time, however, and Desdemona is moved by her relatively new love for her older and accomplished husband. She tells Iago that Othello's "unkindness may defeat" her life but not her love.

As the action progresses Emilia moves from playing Iago's dutiful wife to defying him and exposing her husband's deceit. In her conversation with Desdemona in Act IV, Scene 3, Emilia questions the double standard that allows for men's unfaithfulness and not women's. Her rhetorical questions concerning why men treat women as they do illustrate her main contention that wives have the same foibles as their husbands. In the final scene, Emilia's defiance of Iago and her bravery in telling the truth bring her character to the forefront of the action.

The male characters in *Othello* separate women into categories: either virginal idols (as Cassio worships "divine" Desdemona) or whores (represented by the frequent use of the word *strumpet*). Iago initiates this division in his satiric categorizing of women in Act II, Scene 1, when he accuses them of being duplicitous hussies who play various roles in society. Once Iago convinces Othello that Desdemona has been unfaithful, Othello assigns his wife the role of "strumpet." This misogyny (hatred of women) is emphasized in the scene in which Othello treats both Desdemona and Emilia as whores in a brothel. Before he kills Desdemona, Othello again calls her "strumpet!"—and Iago calls Emilia "villainous whore" before stabbing her to death.

Chronology

1564 William Shakespeare is born on April 23 in Stratford-upon-Avon, England

1578–1582 Span of Shakespeare's "Lost Years," covering the time between leaving school and marrying Anne Hathaway of Stratford

1582 At age eighteen Shakespeare marries Anne Hathaway, age twenty-six, on November 28

1583 Susanna Shakespeare, William and Anne's first child, is born in May, six months after the wedding

1584 Birth of twins Hamnet and Judith Shakespeare

1585–1592 Shakespeare leaves his family in Stratford to become an actor and playwright in a London theater company

1587 Public beheading of Mary Queen of Scots

1593–94 The Bubonic (Black) Plague closes theaters in London

1594–96 As a leading playwright, Shakespeare creates some of his most popular work, including *A Midsummer Night's Dream* and *Romeo and Juliet*

1596 Hamnet Shakespeare dies in August at age eleven, possibly of plague

1596-97	*The Merchant of Venice* and *Henry IV, Part One* most likely are written
1599	The Globe Theater opens
1600	*Julius Caesar* is first performed at the Globe
1600-01	*Hamlet* is believed to have been written
1601-02	*Twelfth Night* is probably composed
1603	Queen Elizabeth dies; Scottish king James VI succeeds her and becomes England's James I
1604	Shakespeare pens *Othello*
1605	*Macbeth* is composed
1608-1610	London's theaters are forced to close when the plague returns and kills an estimated 33,000 people
1611	*The Tempest* is written
1613	The Globe Theater is destroyed by fire
1614	Reopening of the Globe
1616	Shakespeare dies on April 23
1623	Anne Hathaway, Shakespeare's widow, dies; a collection of Shakespeare's plays, known as the First Folio, is published

Source Notes

Page 28, par. 1, Edward Pechter made this comment in *Othello and Interpretive Traditions.* (Pechter 1999 2).

Page 39, par. 3, Michael Neill discusses Marlowe's *Dr. Faustus* as more of an "influence" on Shakespeare than a "source" in the *Oxford Shakespeare Othello.* (Neill 2006 16–18).

Page 45, par. 4, Commenting on Brabantio's warning, Gerald Eades Bentley discusses the "Elizabethan ideal of respect for parents" and questions whether the Othello who cannot really "see" Iago has really seen Desdemona. (Bentley 1969 1019).

Page 52, par. 5, The Romantic poet Samuel Taylor Coleridge found Iago's attempts to justify his behavior as "the motive-hunting of a motiveless malignity."

Page 53, par. 2, In *A Reader's Guide to Shakespeare,* Alfred Harbage defines nuptial in this scene as "the consummation of marriage." (Harbage 1974 353).

Page 58, par. 3, As early as 1693 the British critic Thomas Rymer found the plot device of the handkerchief one of many "improbabilities" in *Othello.* (Neill 2006 3-5).

Page 60, par. 2, Courtesans (such as Bianca) should not be considered prostitutes in the modern sense. In Venice these women tended to come from the upper class and were usually quite cultured.

Page 66, par. 2, Emilia's reasoning recalls Shylock's argument in *The Merchant of Venice* that wicked Jews learn their dishonest ways from hypocritical Christians.

Page 93, par. 4, The ram's blackness may indicate it is a representation of the devil. (Neill 2006 203).

Page 97, par. 4, The quote from Marowitz's play *An Othello* comes from this Website: http://www.pbs.org/wgbh/masterpiece/othello/tg_race.html

Page 97, par. 5, Michael Neill provides a fine, lengthy discussion of political and artistic responses to *Othello* through the centuries. (Neill 2006 11–16).

A Shakespeare Glossary

The student should not try to memorize these, but only refer to them as needed. We can never stress enough that the best way to learn Shakespeare's language is simply to *hear* it—to hear it spoken well by good actors. After all, small children master every language on earth through their ears, without studying dictionaries, and we should master Shakespeare, as much as possible, the same way.

addition — a name or title (knight, duke, duchess, king, etc.)
admire — to marvel
affect — to like or love; to be attracted to
an — if ("An I tell you that, I'll be hanged.")
approve — to prove or confirm
attend — to pay attention
belike — probably
beseech — to beg or request
betimes — soon; early
bondman — a slave
bootless — futile; useless; in vain
broil — a battle
charge — expense; responsibility; to command or accuse
clepe, clept — to name; named
common — of the common people; below the nobility
conceit — imagination
condition — social rank; quality
countenance — face; appearance; favor
cousin — a relative
cry you mercy — beg your pardon
curious — careful; attentive to detail
dear — expensive
discourse — to converse; conversation
discover — to reveal or uncover
dispatch — to speed or hurry; to send; to kill
doubt — to suspect

entreat — to beg or appeal

envy — to hate or resent; hatred; resentment

ere — before

ever, e'er — always

eyne — eyes

fain — gladly

fare — to eat; to prosper

favor — face, privilege

fellow — a peer or equal

filial — of a child toward its parent

fine — an end; in fine = in sum

fond — foolish

fool — a darling

genius — a good or evil spirit

gentle — well-bred; not common

gentleman — one whose labor was done by servants (Note: to call someone a *gentleman* was not a mere compliment on his manners; it meant that he was above the common people.)

gentles — people of quality

get — to beget (a child)

go to — "go on"; "come off it"

go we — let us go

haply — perhaps

happily — by chance; fortunately

hard by — nearby

heavy — sad or serious

husbandry — thrift; economy

instant — immediate

kind — one's nature; species

knave — a villain; a poor man

lady — a woman of high social rank (Note: *lady* was not a synonym for *woman* or *polite woman*; it was not a compliment, but, like *gentleman*, simply a word referring to one's actual legal status in society.)

leave — permission; "take my leave" = depart (with permission)

lief, lieve — "I had as lief" = I would just as soon; I would rather

like — to please; "it likes me not" = it is disagreeable to me

livery — the uniform of a nobleman's servants; emblem
mark — notice; pay attention
morrow — morning
needs — necessarily
nice — too fussy or fastidious
owe — to own
passing — very
peculiar — individual; exclusive
privy — private; secret
proper — handsome; one's very own ("his proper son")
protest — to insist or declare
quite — completely
require — request
several — different, various;
severally — separately
sirrah — a term used to address social inferiors
sooth — truth
state — condition; social rank
still — always; persistently
success — result(s)
surfeit — fullness
touching — concerning; about; as for
translate — to transform
unfold — to disclose
villain — a low or evil person; originally, a peasant
voice — a vote; consent; approval
vouchsafe — to confide or grant
vulgar — common
want — to lack
weeds — clothing
what ho — "hello, there!"
wherefore — why
wit — intelligence; sanity
withal — moreover; nevertheless
without — outside
would — wish

Suggested Essay Topics

1. Using references and examples from the play, argue for or against this statement: Othello is responsible for his own downfall and the loss of everything that matters to him. Remember to develop a strong thesis statement.

2. Discuss the role that social class plays in *Othello.* How do economics and social standing affect both character behavior and events throughout the play? What effect does social class have on the tragedy that takes place?

3. Discuss the state of race relations in the context of the play. How does race affect both Othello's view of himself and the other characters' views of Othello? Does our modern worldview alter the play's racial aspects?

4. Watch one of the DVDs of *Othello* and write an essay comparing and contrasting the director's interpretation and Shakespeare's play. In light of having read the play closely, discuss what is or is not successful about the performance, including what the director has changed and the actors playing the roles.

5. In a well-developed essay, respond to Emilia's speech in Act IV, Scene 3, about women and men. Emilia claims, "I do think it is their husbands' faults/If wives do fail." Explain and respond to her various arguments throughout her speech to Desdemona.

Testing Your Memory

1. The military rank Iago feels has been stolen from him is:
a) ensign; b) general; c) captain; d) lieutenant.

2. The play's action takes place in two places: Venice and:
a) Verona; b) Cyprus; c) Ceylon; d) London.

3. As a Moor Othello originally comes from:
a) North Africa b) Southeast Asia; c) India; d) South America.

4. Brabantio is Desdemona's:
a) father; b) uncle; c) servant; d) clown.

5. The Venetians have been warring with these people:
a) the Africans; b) the Turks; c) the Florentines; d) the British.

6. This character is accused of using black magic:
a) Othello; b) Brabantio; c) Iago; d) Desdemona.

7. This lovelorn character wants to drown himself:
a) Cassio; b) Othello; c) Roderigo; d) Iago.

8. This character has a problem with drinking alcohol:
a) Cassio; b) Roderigo; c) Othello; d) Clown.

9. This character cries out: "I have lost my reputation!":
a) Cassio; b) Othello; c) Roderigo; d) Iago.

10. Cassio bribes this character:
a) Roderigo; b) Emilia; c) Iago; d) Clown.

11. The person who calls jealousy a "green-eyed monster" is:
a) Emilia; b) Iago; c) Othello; d) Desdemona.

12. This character says about Desdemona: "She did deceive her father, marrying you":   a) Iago; b) Brabantio; c) Roderigo; d) Lodovico.

13. Othello believes Desdemona has been unfaithful with this man:
a) Iago; b) Roderigo; c) Gratiano; d) Cassio.

14. This character finds the handkerchief on the ground:
a) Bianca ; b) Desdemona ; c) Emilia ; d) Othello.

15. The pattern on the handkerchief features these objects:
a) hearts ; b) tears ; c) ships ; d) strawberries.

16. Bianca is:
a) Desdemona's servant; b) Cassio's wife; c) Iago's mistress; d) a courtesan.

17. He asks Bianca to make a copy of the handkerchief:
a) Othello; b) Cassio; c) Iago; d) Roderigo.

18. He stabs and kills Roderigo:
a) Cassio; b) Montano; c) Iago; d) Othello.

19. At the end of the play, Iago is:
a) killed by Lodovico; b) killed by Othello; c) wounded by Lodovico;
d) wounded by Othello.

20. At the end of the play, Othello:
a) is imprisoned; b) is stabbed by Iago; c) is killed by Lodovico; d) stabs
himself and dies.

Answer Key

Further Information

BOOKS

Bloom, Harold. *Shakespeare's Othello.* New York: Riverhead Trade, 2005.

Holte, Gayle, ed. *Othello.* Shakespeare Made Easy. Hauppauge, NY: Barron's, 2002.

Honigmann, E.A.J., Ed. *Othello.* The Arden Shakespeare. London: Arden, 2006.

Shakespeare, William. *The Oxford Shakespeare Othello.* Edited by Michael Neill. Oxford World's Classics. Edited by Stanley Wells. Oxford and New York: Oxford University Press, 2006.

WEBSITES

Absolute Shakespeare. A massive resource offering information on Shakespeare's biography, the plays, summaries, sonnets, quotes, films, and other resources.
www.absoluteshakespeare.com/plays/othello/othello.htm.

Shakespeare-Online. Site offers plot synopsis, sources, character studies, essay topics, and an essay ("Othello Analysis") by Amanda Mabillard.
www.shakespeare-online.com/playanalysis/othello.

DOWNLOAD

William Shakespeare's "Othello": A Study Guide from Gale's "Drama for Students" (Volume 20, Chapter 8). Adobe Reader. 40 pages.

http://www.amazon.com/William-Shakespeares-Othello-Students-Chapter/dp/B0006MS2ES

ENCYCLOPEDIA ENTRY

Shakespeare's World and Work: An Encyclopedia for Students, s.v. "Othello."

Vol. 2. Ed. John F. Andrews. Charles Scribner's Sons: New York, 2001.

FILMS

O. (Mekhi Phifer, Josh Hartnett, Julia Stiles), special ed. DVD. Directed by Tim Blake Nelson. Lion's Gate, 2001. *Othello* reinterpreted as a contemporary high school drama about a basketball player named Odin.

Othello (1995; Laurence Fishburne, Kenneth Branagh). DVD. Directed by Oliver Parker. Turner Home Entertainment, 2000.

Othello (1965; Laurence Olivier, Maggie Smith). DVD. Directed by Stuart Burge and John Dexter. Warner Home Video, 2007.

Othello (Michael Grandage, Ian McKellen). DVD. Directed by Trevor Nunn. Image Entertainment, 2004.

OPERA

Verdi, Giuseppe. *Otello.* Vienna Philharmonic Orchestra. Conducted by Herbert von Karajan. Decca: 2002.

Bibliography

Bentley, Gerald Eades. "Othello the Moor of Venice." *William Shakespeare: The Compete Works.* Edited by Alfred Harbage. Baltimore: Penguin Books, 1969.

Harbage, Alfred. *A Reader's Guide to Shakespeare.* New York: Farrar, Straus and Giroux, 1974.

Neill, Michael. "Introduction." *The Oxford Shakespeare Othello.* Oxford World's Classics. Edited by Stanley Wells. Oxford and New York: Oxford University Press, 2006.

Pechter, Edward. *Othello and Interpretive Traditions.* Iowa City: University of Iowa Press, 1999.

Index

About the Author

Mark Mussari is a freelance writer and educator living in Tucson, Arizona. He has his Ph.D. in Scandinavian Languages and Literature from the University of Washington and taught for a number of years at Villanova University. He is the author of nonfiction books, academic journal articles, encyclopedia entries, and numerous magazine articles on art, design, and entertainment.